END OF COURSE REVIEW

prepared for the course team by
david goldblatt, hugh mackay and gerry mooney

This publication forms part of an Open University course DD100 *An Introduction to the Social Sciences: Understanding Social Change*. Details of this and other Open University courses can be obtained from the Call Centre, PO Box 724, The Open University, Milton Keynes MK7 6ZS, United Kingdom: tel. +44 (0)1908 653231, e-mail ces-gen@open.ac.uk

Alternatively, you may visit the Open University website at http://www.open.ac.uk where you can learn more about the wide range of courses and packs offered at all levels by The Open University.

To purchase this publication or other components of Open University courses, contact Open University Worldwide Ltd, The Berrill Building, Walton Hall, Milton Keynes MK7 6AA, United Kingdom: tel. +44 (0)1908 858785; fax +44 (0)1908 858787; e-mail ouwenq@open.ac.uk; website http://www.ouw.co.uk

The Open University
Walton Hall, Milton Keynes
MK7 6AA

First published 2000. Second edition 2001

Edited, designed and typeset by The Open University.

Printed in the United Kingdom by The Bath Press, Bath.

ISBN 0 7492 7748 3

2.1

10242B/dd100endisbn0749277483i2.1

Contents

The DD100 course team

John Allen, *Senior Lecturer in Geography*

Penny Bennett, *Editor*

Pam Berry, *Compositor*

Simon Bromley, *Senior Lecturer in Government*

David Calderwood, *Project Controller*

Elizabeth Chaplin, *Tutor Panel*

Giles Clark, *Co-publishing Advisor*

Stephen Clift, *Editor*

Allan Cochrane, *Professor of Public Policy*

Lene Connolly, *Print Buying Controller*

Graham Dawson, *Lecturer in Economics*

Lesley Duguid, *Senior Course Co-ordination Secretary*

Fran Ford, *Senior Course Co-ordination Secretary*

David Goldblatt, *Co-Course Team Chair, Lecturer in Government*

Jenny Gove, *Lecturer in Psychology*

Judith Greene, *Professor of Psychology*

Montserrat Guibernau, *Lecturer in Government*

Peter Hamilton, *Lecturer in Sociology*

Celia Hart, *Picture Researcher*

David Held, *Professor of Politics and Sociology*

Susan Himmelweit, *Senior Lecturer in Economics*

Steve Hinchliffe, *Lecturer in Geography*

Anne Howells, *Project Controller*

Gordon Hughes, *Lecturer in Social Policy*

Christina Janoszka, *Course Manager*

Pat Jess, *Staff Tutor in Geography (Region 12)*

Bob Kelly, *Staff Tutor in Government (Region 06)*

Margaret Kiloh, *Staff Tutor in Applied Social Sciences (Region 13)*

Sylvia Lay-Flurrie, *Secretary*

Siân Lewis, *Graphic Designer*

Tony McGrew, *Professor of International Relations, University of Southampton*

Hugh Mackay, *Staff Tutor in Sociology (Region 10)*

Maureen Mackintosh, *Professor of Economics*

Eugene McLaughlin, *Senior Lecturer in Applied Social Science*

Andrew Metcalf, *Senior Producer, BBC*

Gerry Mooney, *Staff Tutor in Applied Social Sciences (Region 11)*

Ray Munns, *Graphic Artist*

Kathy Pain, *Staff Tutor in Geography (Region 02)*

Clive Pearson, *Tutor Panel*

Lynne Poole, *Tutor Panel*

Norma Sherratt, *Staff Tutor in Sociology (Region 03)*

Roberto Simonetti, *Lecturer in Economics*

Dick Skellington, *Project Officer*

Brenda Smith, *Staff Tutor in Psychology (Region 12)*

Mark Smith, *Lecturer in Social Sciences*

Grahame Thompson, *Professor of Political Economy*

Ken Thompson, *Professor of Sociology*

Stuart Watt, *Lecturer in Psychology/KMI*

Andy Whitehead, *Graphic Artist*

Kath Woodward, *Co-Course Team Chair, Staff Tutor in Sociology (Region 07)*

Chris Wooldridge, *Editor*

External Assessor

Nigel Thrift, *Professor of Geography, University of Bristol*

1 INTRODUCTION

1.1 Block overview

Almost there. Your work on Block 6 will occupy the last three weeks of your study time on DD100 and then you are done (as ever, the course materials and recommended route are detailed below, Figures 1 and 2). The structure and purpose of Block 6 is very similar to the Mid Course Review which you studied a couple of months ago. The block is structured around a discussion of the changing character of the city in post-Second World War UK. This discussion serves as a trigger and a device for you to revisit the earlier blocks of the course, and provides an opportunity for thinking through the course themes and their development right the way across the blocks. The course themes provide the subject matter for the final TMA of the course, TMA 06.

Study week	Course material	Suggested study time
31 and 32	*End of Course Review* Audio-cassette 10, Sides A and B	23 hours 1 hour
33	TMA 06	12 hours

FIGURE 1 Course materials for Block 6

BOX 1   **Your study route for Block 6**

Please note, the study route in Figure 2 is only the recommended route through the materials. This review is over 160 pages long and while working through all of it will allow you to consolidate your studies across the whole course we recognize that, in the final weeks of your study, time is pressing. So, please note, that while Sections 1 and 2 of the review are virtually obligatory, you need only study one of Sections 3 to 5 in depth – you will not be penalized in any way for looking at just one section. More advice on what to do, and which section or sections to choose, will be coming on Audio-cassette 10, Side A at the end of Section 2.

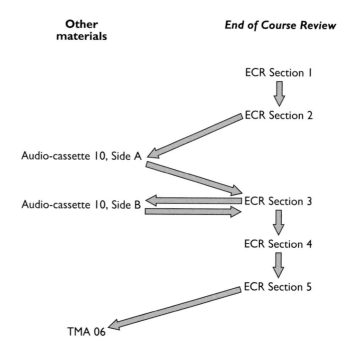

FIGURE 2
Recommended study
route for Block 6
(see also Box 1)

1.2 Key questions, key skills

The main purpose of Block 6 is to give you an opportunity to synthesize, sift and integrate materials right the way across DD100. So, the key skill that drives your work in Block 6 is one that you worked on in Block 5 – *synthesis and integration* (see *Workbook 5*, pp.12–13). In addition, you will find yourself drawing upon a whole range of other skills that you have developed through the course: reading maps, visual images and evidence; constructing, comparing and evaluating arguments; etc.

Our starting point for this process is an account of the city in the post-war UK and a series of questions about the city. In Section 2 of the *End of Course Review* we will be asking you to think about the relationship between the city and the key themes of the main blocks of DD100. We will be asking a series of questions about the relationship between the city and identity, the city and the natural, the city and power, etc. This will also give you an opportunity to begin going over your notes from the earlier parts of the course, reducing them, focusing them and, above all, using them. It is also an opportunity to develop your reading skills as we will be presenting you with a number of edited readings from contemporary social science research on the city. You have already encountered some writing like this in the readings in earlier parts of the course. On future courses in the social sciences you will encounter a lot more, so Block 6 gets you started on the skills of reading it and using it.

In Sections 3–5 of the *End of Course Review* we will be asking you to build on this work by looking at the relationship between the city in the post-war UK and the course themes.

- Section 3 constructs a broad narrative account of the changes in the post-war city structured by our notions of *uncertainty and diversity.*

- Section 4 focuses on the experience of change in one city – Cardiff – as a way of exploring the interaction of *structure and agency* in urban change.

- Section 5 looks at the changing relationship between cities and information and knowledge in the post-war UK and asks how, as social scientists, we can understand, explain and evaluate that relationship. So, Section 5 draws on both the analytical and narrative strands of *knowledge and knowing.*

In each section the discussion of the city will provide a starting point for a series of exercises and ideas that draw on materials from right the way across the course.

1.3 Assessing Block 6

As with the rest of DD100 all of this will be assessed in a TMA. In this case, it is TMA 06. We will be asking you to write a 1,500 word essay that explores **one** of the course themes. You will be able to choose from three questions. We will, in addition, ask you to draw on material from at least three of Blocks 1–6. More detail on what to do and how to do it will be available in your student notes for TMA 06. Audio-cassette 10, Side A is a conversation between course team members, with ideas and suggestions for how to plan your time and get started on these tasks.

2 CITY THEMES

The purposes of this section are three-fold:

- To introduce you to some key ideas and debates about the city in the social sciences, in connection with each of the five main blocks of the course. These debates will be further explored in Sections 3–5 of the *End of Course Review*, focusing more closely on the city in the post-war UK.

- To develop your skills of consolidating and reflecting on materials you have already studied by looking back to the work you did in Blocks 1–5.

- To develop your skills of synthesizing and integrating by exploring the connections between the material on the city and your own notes on each of the main blocks of DD100.

You may, before continuing, want to look back to some earlier parts of the course where these skills have been discussed and some key techniques have been explored. In particular:

- *Introductory Workbook*, Section 7 on *reflection*.

- *Workbook 3*, see the summary in Section 6 on *revision skills*.

You will also need your own notes and summaries from the earlier blocks to hand as you work through the following sections.

2.1 The city and identity

What kinds of connections and relationships between the city and identity can you think of? Jot down any notes or ideas you have.

Our brainstorm came up with two basic ideas:

- Cities provide a source of identity, belonging, community – people are Glaswegians, Londoners, Mancunians, etc. See Book 1, Chapter 4, Sections 1 and 2 on the role of place and identity formation.

- Cities shape and reflect the formation and character of other identities. The geography of most cities, such as the Belfast example in Book 1, Chapter 4, Section 1, is socially stratified: by class, ethnicity, etc.

Before we start connecting up these points about the city with the material in Block 1 of the course, we want to explore the relationship between cities and identity a bit further.

A C T I V I T Y   I

Read the extracts below from Jonathan Raban's *Soft City*.

How does Raban characterize the relationship between the city and identity? *wherever.*

What makes the city different from villages and small towns? *Column*

Jonathan Raban: 'Soft city'

The Soft City

I come out of a formica kebab-house alone after lunch, my head prickly with retsina. The air outside is a sunny swirl of exhaust fumes; that faint, smoky-turquoise big city colour. I stand on the pavement waiting to cross at the lights. Suddenly I know that I don't know the direction of the traffic. Do cars here drive on the left or the right hand side of the road? A cluster of Italian au pair girls, their voices mellow and labial, like a chorus escaped from an opera, pass me; I hear, in the crowd, an adenoidal Nebraskan contralto, twangy as a jew's-harp. Turned to a dizzied tourist myself, forgetful and jet-shocked, I have to hunt in my head for the language spoken here.

— country?

But this is where you live; it's your city – London, or New York, or wherever – and its language is the language you've always known, the language from which *being you, being me,* are inseparable. In those dazed moments at stop-lights, it's possible to be a stranger to yourself, to be so doubtful as to who you are that you have to check on things like the placards round the news-vendors' kiosks or the uniforms of the traffic policemen. You're a balloonist adrift, and you need anchors to tether you down.

— language.

A sociologist, I suppose, would see these as classic symptoms of alienation, more evidence to add to the already fat dossier on the evils of urban life. I feel more hospitable towards them. For at moments like this, the city goes soft; it awaits the imprint of an identity. For better or worse, it invites you to remake it, to consolidate it into a shape you can live in. You, too. Decide who you are, and the city will again assume a fixed form round you. Decide what it is, and your own identity will be revealed, like a position on a map fixed by triangulation. Cities, unlike villages and small towns, are plastic by nature. We mould them in our images: they, in their turn, shape us by the resistance they offer when we try to impose our own personal form on them. In this sense, it seems to me that living in cities is an art, and we need the vocabulary of art, of style, to describe the peculiar relationship between man and material that exists in the continual creative play of urban living. The city as we imagine it, the soft city of illusion, myth, aspiration, nightmare, is as real, maybe more real, than the hard city one can locate on maps in statistics, in monographs on urban sociology and demography and architecture.

Yet the hard facts of cities tend to be large, clear and brutal. A hundred years ago they were the facts of appalling poverty, grimly documented by outside observers like Henry Mayhew, Charles Booth, and, a little later in America, Jacob Riis. Today the overwhelming fact of life in New York, if not in London is the violence brewing in its streets. Indeed, poverty and violence are clearly related: both are primarily dependent on the attitudes people hold towards strangers. The indifference that generates the one, and the hatred that animates the other, stem from the same root feeling. If a city can estrange you from yourself, how much more powerfully can it detach you from the lives of other people, and how deeply immersed you may become in the inaccessibly private community of your own head. [...]

Coming out of the London Underground at Oxford Circus one afternoon, I saw a man go berserk in the crowd on the stairs. 'You fucking ... fucking bastards!' he shouted, and his words rolled round and round the lavatorial porcelain tube as we ploughed through. He was in a neat city suit, with a neat city paper neatly folded in a pink hand. His fingernails were clipped to the quick. What was surprising was that nobody showed surprise: a slight speeding-up in the pace of the crowd, a turned head or two, a quick grimace, but that was all. I think we all knew, could feel on our own pulses, the claustrophobia and the hostility that was eating away at the man who was cursing us. Inside, we were all cursing each other. Who feels love for his fellow-man at rush hour? Not me. I suspect that the best insurance against urban violence is the fact that most of us shrink from contact with strangers; we don't want to touch one another or feel that close to the stink of someone else's life. The muggers and the men who feel-up girls on crowded subway trains are exceptions. But if our unexpressed loathing for strangers in a crowd were to break that barrier of physical inhibition, who knows what hell might be let loose on the streets and underground. [...]

In cities, we have good reason to shrink from strangers. High rates of murder and assault are not in themselves symptoms of urban congestion. A remote, low-density rural area like Cardiganshire in West Wales can more than hold its own against London in its per capita murder figures. But in rural areas the majority of the victims of violent crime know their assailants (indeed, are probably married to them); in cities, the killer and the mugger come out of the anonymous dark, their faces unrecognised, their motives obscure. In a city, you can be known, envied, hated by strangers. In your turn, you can feel the exaggerated, operatic emotions that the city arouses in its inhabitants. [...]

To live in a city is to live in a community of people who are strangers to each other. You have to act on hints and fancies, for they are all that the mobile and cellular nature of city life will allow you. You expose yourself in, and are exposed to by others, fragments, isolated signals, bare disconnected gestures, jungle cries and whispers that resist all your attempts to unravel their meaning, their consistency. As urban dwellers, we live in a world marked by the people at the next table ('Such a brute, that man. She went to the *Seychelles*', comes the sudden loud phrase, breaking out of the confidential murmur), the man glimpsed in the street with a bowler hat and a hacksaw and never seen again, the girl engrossed in her orgasm across the air-well. So much takes place in the head, so little is known and fixed. Signals, styles, systems of rapid, highly-conventionalised communication, are the lifeblood of the big city. [...] The city, our great modern form, is soft, amenable to a dazzling and libidinous variety of lives, dreams, interpretations. But the very plastic qualities which makes the city the great liberator of human identity also cause it to be especially vulnerable to psychosis and totalitarian nightmare. If it can, in the Platonic ideal, be the highest expression of man's reason and sense of his own community with other men, the city can also be a violent, sub-realist, expression of his panic, his envy, his hatred of strangers, his callousness. It's easy to 'drop' people in the city, where size and anonymity and the absence of clear communal sanctions license the kind of behaviour that any village would stamp out at birth. Just as the city is the place where you can choose your society, so it is also the place where you can 'drop' discarded friends, old lovers, the duller members of your family: you can, too, 'drop' the poor, the minorities, the immigrants, everyone, in fact, who isn't to your taste or of your class. The mugger can step out of the shadows to drop a victim who has been singled out by the dimly seen cut of his clothes. In the city we can change our identities at will. [...]

The Magical City

Living in a city, one finds oneself unconsciously slipping into magical habits of mind. As I have tried to show in earlier chapters, surfaces are in any case of enormous importance to the city dweller: he has to learn to respond to a daily cascade of people and places in terms of briefly-exhibited signs and badges. His imagination is always being stretched. In a junky antique shop, I stop bargaining over what might be a late Georgian chair because the man selling it is wearing a navy-blue peaked Carnaby Street cap; his hair, dyed silver grey, curls coyly in ringlets round its rim. Just that hat and those curls make up a message, and I do not trust it; it belongs to the area of the grammar used by sharpies and plausible perfumed frauds. I know next to nothing about Georgian chairs, but the cap and curls are part of the everyday language of the city, and I understand – believe I understand – them as well as if I had actually seen the man spraying woodworm holes into the furniture with a sawn-off shotgun. All the time, one is isolating such details and acting upon them as if they were epigrams. Only rarely is one able to put one's assumptions to the test, to discover incongruities between people and the badges which they wear; and one has to believe, however erroneously in fact, that people behave 'in character', and to trust one's own powers as an interpreter of symbols. For me, this gives city life a curiously vertiginous feeling; I move on the streets always a little apprehensive that the whole slender crust of symbolic meaning might give way under my feet. At the same time I collect more and more signs, a jackdaw's nest of badges and trinkets, continually elaborating the code which I use for deciphering my own world. When new cars come out of motor shows, I watch who buys them: who wears platform heels, buys *Time Out* or *Spare Rib*, ostentatiously sports Harrods carrier bags? [...]

More than that, we map the city by private benchmarks which are meaningful only to us. The Greater London Council is responsible for a sprawl shaped like a rugby ball about twenty five miles long and twenty miles wide; my city is a concise kidney-shaped patch within that space, in which no point is more than about seven miles from any other. On the South, it is bounded by the river, on the north by the fat tongue of Hampstead Heath and Highgate Village, on the west by Brompton cemetery and on the east by Liverpool Street station. I hardly ever trespass beyond those limits, and when I do I feel I'm in foreign territory, a landscape of hazard and rumour. Kilburn, on the far side of my northern and western boundaries, I imagine to be inhabited by vicious drunken Irishmen; Hackney and Dalston by crooked car dealers with pencil moustaches and goldfilled teeth; London south of the Thames still seems impossibly illogical and contingent, a territory of meaningless circles, incomprehensible one-way systems, warehouses and cage-bird shops. Like any tribesman hedging himself in behind a stockade of taboos, I mark my boundaries with graveyards, terminal transportation points and wildernesses. Beyond them, nothing is to be trusted and anything might happen.

The constrictedness of this private city-within-a-city has the character of a self-fulfilling prophecy. Its boundaries, originally arrived at by chance and usage, grow more not less real the longer I live in London. I have friends who live in Clapham, only three miles away, but to visit them is a definite journey, for it involves crossing the river. I can, though, drop in on friends in Islington, twice as far away as Clapham, since it is within what I feel to be my own territory. When I first came to London, I moved about the city much more freely than I do now; I took the liberties of a tourist and measured distances in miles rather than by the relationship of the known to the unknown. [...] It is the visitor who goes everywhere; to the resident, a river or a railway track, even if it is bridged every few hundred yards, may be as absolute a boundary as a snakepit or an ocean.

Inside one's private city, one builds a grid of reference points, each enshrining a personal attribution of meaning. A black-fronted bookshop in South Kensington, a line of gothic balconies on the Cromwell Road, a devastated recreation ground between Holloway and Camden, a café full of Polish exiles playing chess in Hampstead, a shop window stuffed with Chinese kitsch, illuminated sampans and revolving perspex table lamps with tassels, in Gerrard Street – these [...] symbols, each denoting a particular quarter, become as important as tube stations. And the underground railway itself turns into an object of superstition. People who live on the Northern Line I take to be sensitive citizens; it is a friendly communication route where one notices commuters reading proper books and, when they talk, finishing their sentences. But the Piccadilly Line is full of fly-by-nights and stripe-shirted young men who run dubious agencies, and I go to elaborate lengths to avoid travelling on it. It is an entirely irrational way of imposing order on the city, but it does give it a shape in the mind, takes whole chunks of experience out of the realm of choice and deliberation, and places them in the less strenuous context of habit and prejudice [...] I avoid walking on cracks between the paving stones, I count lamp posts in units of seven, at zebra crossings I am especially wary of every third vehicle. From my study window, I see people surreptitiously touching the spikes of the house-railings in some occult combination of their own. In London, postal districts, though often thinly related to the changes of character in individual areas, have been endowed with curiously absolutist values.

Prestigious ones, like SW1, SW3, NW1, NW3, are like talismans, more important even than the house or the street, magical guarantees of a certain kind of identity.

These are small, perhaps trivial, rituals, but they do suggest that there is rather more than a merely vestigial magicality in the way we deal with the cities we live in. It is precisely because the city is too large and formless to be held in the mind as an imaginative whole that we make recourse to irrational short-cuts and simplifications. Magic may be a major alternative to rejection of the city as a bad unmanageable place; it offers a real way of surviving in an environment whose rationale has, like a dead language, become so obscure that only a handful of specialists (alas, they are all too frequently sociologists, urban economists and town planners) can remember or understand it. The rest of us make do with an improvised day-to-day magic which, like shamanism, works because we conspire that it shall work.

Source: Raban, 1974, pp.9–16, 165–9

COMMENT

Our notes looked like this:

THE SOFT CITY

Moments of uncertainty in city – example of alienation or...

Moment of uncertainty – city becomes soft/pliable – shaped by, given meaning and order by individuals, but limits to that shaping. Cities in turn shape us, our identities.

> 'Cities, unlike villages and small towns, are plastic by nature. We mould them in our images: they, in their turn, shape us by the resistance they offer'.

But cities shaped by violence, poverty and attitudes to strangers – cities make oneself and others strange/distant/fearful. NB Murder rates in the country can be as high but attackers known. (Is this backed up by evidence?)

City life structured by tensions:

1 Between physical closeness of others and fear, anonymity of others, i.e. man on the tube.

2 Between possibility of liberation, choice of new identities, threat and panic of losing one's identity, being dropped by others.

THE MAGICAL CITY

Consequence of living with strangers/uncertainty – need for city dweller to be expert in reading fleeting signs, roles, etc. – grasping other people's identity and motivations from the outside, i.e. the chair-buying example.

City dwellers construct their own sense of space/maps of the city (see the discussion of mental maps in Study Skills Supplement 3).

Again soft city (mental map) contrasted with physical/hard city (underground map).

What does Raban add to our brainstorm? He doesn't say much about the city as a source of collective identity, but, perhaps as a consequence, he has a great deal to say about the city and individual identities. In particular:

- He offers an account of what makes a city a distinctive place – the tensions between proximity and distance, intimacy and alienation.

- He distinguishes between the hard city (material structures, physical infrastructure) and the soft city (mental, cultural and symbolic worlds).

- He argues that the soft city is central to, indeed invites, individual identity formation. This makes for liberating possibilities of self-creation and transformation, but also holds out the threat of fragmentation, neurosis, and alienation – so agency is particularly significant in making these identities.

So, combining these points we came up with Diagram A. This is one way of representing ideas in note form which some students find useful.

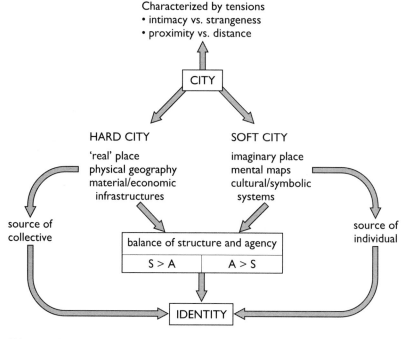

Diagram A

Now we are going to try and connect this material to the work you did on identity in Block 1 of the course and alert you to the places in the rest of this review where we return to the city and identity. The first step is to go back to the contents of Block 1.

ACTIVITY 2

Look back over your notes on Block 1. If you have not collected them together or reduced them, take the opportunity now to have a go.

You may want to work with the questions and techniques we suggest below.

However you go about doing this, please, please do it yourself first. Our attempt below is for discussion and comparison. These notes are not definitive or comprehensive, nor do they necessarily reflect your understanding of the course. We cannot emphasize enough that you will only prepare yourself properly for TMA 06 by making your own notes.

Questions:

- What were the key questions of the block?
- In what ways were the course themes used? What kinds of questions did they raise?
- In what ways did each chapter in the block address these issues? What were the key debates in each chapter? What different or opposing perspectives were used to explore the materials?
- What were the key case studies, the best examples, and the types of empirical evidence used?
- What additional materials from the audio-cassettes and the TV programme can you use?

Techniques:

- Skim your own notes and/or the Introductions and Afterwords to the main textbooks.
- Skim the introductory sections to the workbooks, your own notes and efforts on key summarizing activities in the workbooks (grids, tables, diagrammatic notes), and any work you did in connection with the consolidation and reflection section of each workbook.
- Skim and note the summaries of each chapter. Better still, use your own notes for this.

COMMENT _____

Our quick notes looked like this:

QUESTIONS

1 How are identities formed?

2 Extent we can shape identities?

3 Uncertainty about identity?

THEMES

U+D

Are identities more complex, diverse; decline in stereotypes, emergence of new and multiple identities?

Uncertainties around Britishness/masculinity, old models of class society.

S+A

Explores relative weight S+A in identity formation.
Different structures – social, biological, cultural, political, and economic.

Recognizes individual agency, collective agency – nations, new social movements, etc.

K+K

Question-driven social science.

Introduction to circuit of knowledge in workbook, Sect. 1.4.

CHAPTERS AND DEBATES

Ch. 1

Concept of identity.

Mead, Goffman and Freud.

Althusser and social structures.

Ch. 2

Sex and gender.

Role biological, social structures.

Problem of fuzzy categories.

Theory self-categorization.

Impact of gender identities on school performance – Murphy and Elwood.

Ch. 3

Understands economic structures in terms of poverty, income, work, and wealth.

Marx vs. Weber models of stratification.

Work vs. consumption as source of identity.

Social polarization vs. social fragmentation.

Ch. 4

Relationship identity and place - cities, nations.

Conceptual relationship - nations, states, nation-states, ethnicity.

National identities shaped by cultural, geographical, economic and political structures, and conscious agency.

Explanations of nationalism - Gellner vs. Anderson vs. Smith.

Civic vs. ethnic nationalism.

EVIDENCE AND EXAMPLES

Ch. 1

Sarup; passport.

Greaves - autobiographical writing.

Kay - poem.

Ch. 2

Bem's Sex Role Inventory test.

Conversational and observational analysis of children.

Statistical data on exam performance.

Observation of classroom practice.

Ch. 3

Statistical evidence on wealth, poverty, income.

Interviews with people on low income.

Case study of call centres.

Ch. 4

Belfast example.

Cenotaph rituals.

Scotland as case study.

England as case study.

AUDIO AND TV

TV 01 - Diana and Churchill, contrast in representation and sense
of Britishness, decline of old elites, new populism and diversity,
role of mass media.

How did your notes compare with ours?

Let us emphasize again: **you should not be producing comprehensive notes
or notes identical to ours.**

What you should be producing is a set of notes that you can use to help you
prepare for TMA 06, which will require you to draw on material from at least
three of Blocks 1–6. You may find it useful to have a look at the TMA booklet
now, it will be clearer what kinds of materials connected to what issues you
will need to be looking out for.

You may find that you have too many notes or that our suggestions for
organizing the material are unhelpful or that the whole process is proving
rather fraught. If so:

1   Take a look at Box 2 which lays out one model of generating
    condensed notes from course materials.

2   Call your tutor or other students you are in contact with to
    discuss it.

3   Have another go at taking shorter, sharper notes from your first
    notes.

BOX 2   Condensing your notes

Is it worth writing new notes at this stage in the course?

Yes, it is an excellent idea to work with a pen in your hand, actually _creating_
something as you work! This gives a much more constructive feel to the tasks
of revision and synthesis and will engage your mind more effectively for
long spells of work. One way of working which some students find useful is as
follows:

Make _very condensed notes_ from various books, notes, etc. that you have
gathered together for revision on a particular topic.

Then extract the main points from these condensed notes to produce a
single _summary sheet_ of headings with key points, names, etc. for that
topic.

Finally, having done this for the topics within a given section of the course,
take the main headings from all the topic summary sheets and produce a
single _master summary sheet_ which outlines the main subject matter for that
whole _section_ of the course.

The effort to 'boil' the course down in this way, so as to extract its concentrated essence, is extremely valuable because it converts the broad themes and the detailed discussions of the course into a form which is much more manageable for the purposes of writing TMA 06 and, on future courses, for answering questions in exams.

What is more, when you come to answering TMA 06, you can remind yourself of the *key points summary sheet*, to identify what main topics lie within the section. You then work out which of the topics are relevant to the question and remind yourself of the *topic summary sheets* concerned. You scan mentally through the main items on any given topic summary sheet and select whichever are relevant. This then leads you back towards the condensed notes which 'lie behind' those items on the topic summary sheet. In other words, having, in your revision, constructed pathways *down* from the basic source materials through condensed notes and topic summary sheets to a master summary sheet, you can then quickly trace your way back *up* those pathways, to locate exactly the material that is relevant to the question. Perhaps the practice is rarely quite as neat as that, but at least this 'note-condensing' approach gives you the basis for a systematic over-viewing and retrieval system.

Furthermore, a strategy such as this gives you a well-focused and absorbing task to be getting on with, rather than the aimless scanning back over old material which sends you to sleep and dulls your spirits. And finally, condensed notes will supply you with just the kind of 'pulled together' version of the course which will be invaluable in the future, when you want to remind yourself of what the course was about.

Source: adapted from Northedge, 1990, pp.221–3

The task now is to connect your revision of Block 1 and identity to debates about the city.

Look back at Diagram A above. How would you add material from your revision notes on to this diagram?

Firstly, we thought that we could consider the city in a similar way to class, gender and ethnicity; as a source of identity they drew upon and combined different types of social structure – both physical and material structures – such as geography and place, economic and political relations, and patterns of stratification, and more the symbolic structures of culture, representations and signs.

Secondly, we thought the debate over structure and agency in Block 1 was paralleled by the discussion in the Raban piece (Reading 1) and that some of the accounts of identity formation in Block 1 would be enriched by an encounter with the city.

Thirdly, we thought the theme of uncertainty and diversity was reflected in the Raban piece – though not exhaustively.

Fourthly, there were a number of areas where the gaps in Raban's account of identity formation were fleshed out by Block 1 – greater attention to the consequences of identity formation – especially collective identity and political and social organization.

Diagrammatically we came up with Diagram B.

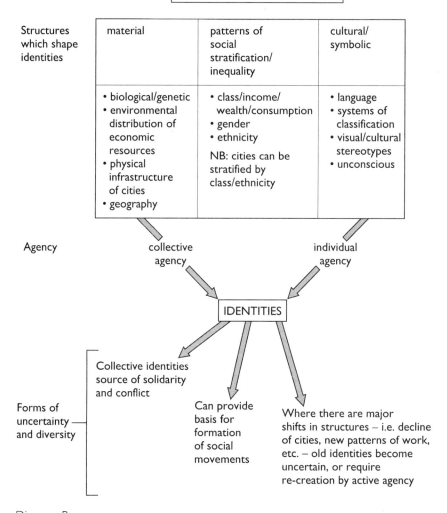

Diagram B

At the end of each sub-section of Section 2 we will be doing our own bit of condensing, highlighting the key issues that will be used, picked upon and developed in Sections 3–5 of the *End of Course Review*. You could take the chance now to:

- Make sure you understand each of the points raised.
- Decide whether you disagree with any of them.
- Note any points of your own that we have missed or insufficiently developed, especially relevant links to Block 1.

SUMMARY

The city and identity.

- Cities are a source of both collective and individual identities.
- Cities are characterized by uniformity and diversity, proximity and distance, intimacy and alienation.
- City identities combine with, and shape, other identities – ethnic, class and gender.
- Cities can be places of uncertainty and uncertain identities.
- Cities can be thought of as a complex amalgamation of structures – hard/soft, material/immaterial, economic, cultural, etc. These structures both shape identities and provide the context for, and possibility of, conscious active agency and choice in identity formation.

2.2 The city, and the natural and the social

What kinds of connections and relationships between the city and the debates about the natural and the social in Block 2 can you think of? Jot down any notes or ideas you have.

Our brainstorm came up with:

1 The city is often counterposed to the countryside. What defines a city is that it is not the country and vice versa.

2 The city is often thought of as something social, humanly created, and the countryside as something natural and not made by humans.

3 But, note the discussion of landscape in Book 2's Introduction, which argues that the countryside/landscape is invariably made and shaped by human activities and that the city invariably contains within it fragments of old ecosystems and new webs of relationships between human beings and micro-organisms, other flora and fauna.

4 Cities, as sites of production and consumption, may be one cause of environmental problems elsewhere as well as within.

ACTIVITY 3

Read the extract below and make short notes that expand upon our initial questions and points.

Richard Rogers: 'Cities as ecosystems'

Cities themselves must be viewed as ecological systems and this attitude must inform our approach to designing cities and managing their use of resources. The resources devoured by a city may be measured in terms of its 'ecological footprint' – an area, scattered throughout the world and vastly greater than the physical boundary of the city itself, on which a city depends. These footprints supply the cities' resources and provide sites for the disposal of their waste and pollution. The ecological footprints of existing cities already virtually cover the entire globe. As the new consumerist cities expand so competition for these resource footprints grow. The expansion of urban ecological footprints is taking place simultaneously with the erosion of fertile lands, living seas and virgin rain forests. Given this simple supply constraint, urban ecological footprints must be dramatically reduced and circumscribed.

The urban ecologist Herbert Girardet has argued that the key lies in cities aiming at a circular 'metabolism', where consumption is reduced by implementing efficiencies and where re-use of resources is maximised. We must recycle materials, reduce waste, conserve exhaustible energies and tap into renewable ones. Since the large majority of production and consumption takes place in cities, current linear processes that create pollution from production must be replaced by those that aim at a circular system of use and re-use. These processes increase a city's overall efficiency and reduce its impact on the environment. To achieve this, we must plan our cities to manage their use of resources, and to do this we need to develop a new form of comprehensive holistic urban planning [...]

Environmental issues are not distinct from social ones. Policies aimed at improving the environment can also improve the social life of citizens. Ecological and social solutions reinforce each other and build healthier, livelier, more open-minded cities. Above all, sustainability means a good life for future generations.

Linear metabolism cities consume and pollute at a high rate

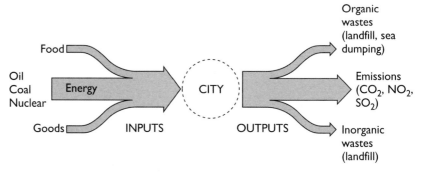

Circular metabolism cities minimise new inputs and maximise recycling

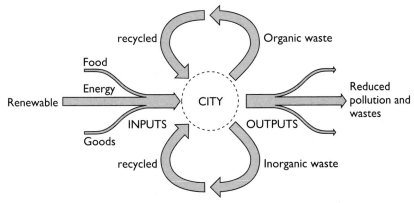

My own approach to urban sustainability reinterprets and reinvents the 'dense city' model. It is worth remembering why, in this century, this model was so categorically rejected. The industrial cities of the nineteenth century were hell: they suffered extremes of overcrowding, poverty and ill-health. Stinking open sewers spread cholera and typhoid; toxic industries stood side by side with overflowing tenements. As a result, life expectancy in many of the industrial cities of Victorian England was less than twenty-five years. It was precisely these hazards and basic inequities that led planners like Ebenezer Howard in 1898, and Patrick Abercrombie in 1944, to propose decanting populations into less dense and greener surroundings: Garden Cities and New Towns.

Today, by contrast, dirty industry is disappearing from cities of the developed world. In theory at least, with the availability of 'green' manufacturing, virtually clean power generation and public transport systems, and advanced sewerage and waste systems, the dense city model need not be seen as a health hazard. This means we can reconsider the social advantages of proximity, rediscover the advantages of living in each other's company.

Beyond social opportunity the 'dense city' model can bring major ecological benefits. Dense cities can through integrated planning be designed to increase energy efficiency, consume fewer resources, produce less pollution and avoid sprawling over the countryside. It is for these reasons that I believe we should be investing in the idea of a 'Compact City' – a dense and socially diverse city where economic and social activities overlap and where communities are focused around neighbourhoods.

This concept differs radically from today's dominant urban model, that of the United States: a city zoned by function with downtown office areas, out-of-town shopping and leisure centres, residential suburbs and highways. So powerful is this image and so prevalent are the forces that motivate its creation (set by the market-driven criteria of commercial developers) that the less developed countries are now locked into a trajectory that has already failed the developed countries.

The pursuit of this approach is having quantifiably disastrous results. The reason for its continued adoption is economic expediency. If the compact and overlapping approach embraces complexity, the zoned approach rejects it, reducing the city to simplistic divisions and easily managed legal and economic packages. Even at the scale of individual buildings, developers both public and private are turning their backs on the concept of mixed use. Traditional city buildings, in which studios sit over family homes, which sit over offices, which sit over shops, bring life to the street and reduce the need for citizens to get into their cars to meet everyday needs. But these mixed-use buildings create complex tenancies which local authorities find hard to manage and developers find hard to finance and sell. Instead, public and private developers prefer single-function buildings. And when embarking on major projects they prefer large open site or cheap 'green-field' ones which offer the possibility of constructing whole housing estates or business parks with minimal leasehold complications. Furthermore, these sites facilitate maximum standardisation of design and construction, thus furthering cost-effectiveness and the argument against mixed-use. The search for short-term profit and quick results continues to turn investment away from complex mixed-use urban development and its inherent social and environmental benefits.

But it is the car which has played the critical role in undermining the cohesive social structure of the city. There are an estimated 500 million cars in the world today. They have eroded the quality of public spaces and have encouraged suburban sprawl. Just as the elevator made the skyscraper possible, so the car has enabled citizens to live away from city centres. The car has made viable the whole concept of dividing everyday activities into compartments, segregating offices, shops and homes. And the wider cities spread out, the more uneconomic it becomes to expand their public transport systems, and the more car-dependent citizens become. Cities around the world are being transformed to facilitate the car even though it is cars rather than industry that are now generating the largest amount of air pollution, the very same pollution that the suburban dwellers are fleeing. [...]

The creation of the modern Compact City demands the rejection of single-function development and the dominance of the car. The question is how to design cities in which communities thrive and mobility is increased – how to design for personal mobility without allowing the car to undermine communal life, how to design for and accelerate the use of clean transport systems and re-balance the use of our streets in favour of the pedestrian and the community.

The Compact City addresses these issues. It grows around centres of social and commercial activity located at public transport nodes. These provide the focal points around which neighbourhoods develop. The Compact City is a network of these neighbourhoods, each with its own parks and public spaces and accommodating a diversity of overlapping private and public activities. London's historic structure of towns, villages, squares and parks is typical of a polycentric pattern of development. Most importantly, these neighbourhoods bring work and facilities within convenient reach of the community, and this proximity means less driving for everyday needs. In large cities, Mass Transit Systems can provide high-speed cross-town travel by linking one neighbourhood centre with another, leaving local distribution to local systems.

This reduces the volume and impact of through traffic, which can be calmed and controlled, particularly around the public heart of neighbourhoods. Local trams, light railway systems and electric buses become more effective, and cycling and walking more pleasant. Congestion and pollution in the streets are drastically reduced and the sense of security and conviviality of public space is increased. [...]

Proximity, the provision of good public space, the presence of natural landscape and the exploitation of new urban technologies can radically improve the quality of air and of life in the dense city. Another benefit of compactness is that the countryside itself is protected from the encroachment of urban development. I will show how the concentration of diverse activities, rather than the grouping of similar activities, can make for more efficient use of energy. The Compact City can provide an environment as beautiful as that of the countryside.

Source: Rogers, 1997, pp.30–8

COMMENT

The core of Rogers' conception of the city challenges our points 1 and 2, and draws upon the notion of the city in 3. He expands our point 4, using the notion of the ecological footprint which reinforces the notion that the countryside is shaped by social forces. So, adapting his diagrams in Reading 2, we drew Diagram C.

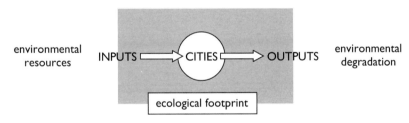

Diagram C

However, Rogers pushes on to offer elements of an explanation of the problem and elements of a solution.

EXPLANATION

Using US model of cities has created:

    linear city

    sprawling city

    car-dominated city

    zoned → and therefore loss of diversity

Market-driven city planning produces above plus exclusion.

SOLUTION

New compact model of city.

Cyclical use of resources.

Dense and diverse use patterns.

Public-transport dominated, social regulation of market.

ACTIVITY 4

Look back over your notes on Block 2. If you have not collected them together or reduced them, take the opportunity now to have a go. We are going to work with the same set of questions as we did in Section 2.1, Activity 2.

- What were the key questions of the block?

- In what ways were the course themes used?

- In what ways did each chapter in the block address these issues? What were the key debates in each chapter?

- What were the key case studies, the best examples, and the types of empirical evidence used?

- What additional materials from the audio-cassette and the TV programme can you use?

COMMENT

Our quick notes looked like this:

QUESTIONS

1 How can we best think about the intermixing of the natural and the social?

2 Impact of mixed views of the soc. and nat. in context of environmental uncertainties and risks?

3 How can soc. sci. help us think about 1 and 2?

THEMES

U+D

Diversity of ways of knowing, describing thinking about the soc./nat. – reflected in different and diverse accounts of origins of intelligence, different models of health, origins of disasters.

Uncertainty – rising levels of environmental danger and risk, conflicts over interpretation of risk, possibility of risk society.

S+A

Complex interaction of natural/biological structures (genes, bodies, and environments) with social structures (models of explanation, social interests, etc.) all help structure human behaviour and beliefs. Model of markets strong on relationship by S+A, esp. recreation of S by outcomes of A.

K+K

Narrative strand – changing and diverse knowledge of health, environmental risks.

Analytical strand – use of evidence, interpretation of evidence, variable methods in soc. sci.

Contrasts with natural sciences.

CHAPTERS AND DEBATES

Ch. 1

Three approaches to human intelligence: neo-Darwinian, genetic determinism and Piaget developmental psychology – different balance of S+A, natural and social, conception of what is meant by nat. and soc.

Ch. 2

Four models of health and illness, all different conceptions and weight given to soc. and nat. structures, types of evidence, models of practice (medical science, social model, complementary med. and New Public Health).

Ch. 3

Model of market neo-classical – to explain environmental degradation. Critiques of model – ignorance of externalities, public goods, etc.

Ch. 4

Conflicting models of explaining natural disasters – natural science vs. social science. Conflicting models of interpreting BSE, uncertainties in public reception of science, emergence of a risk society?

EVIDENCE AND EXAMPLES

Ch. 1

Wide range of evidence used by different approaches to intelligence. Statistical correlation of IQ and parentage,

neo-Darwinian reasoning and questionnaires, conversational
analysis of kids' play.

Ch. 2

Different evidence for different models of health. Scientific
method for medical science. Quantitative data on class and
mortality for social model. Qualitative personal reporting for
complementary methods. Risk analysis for New PH.

Ch. 3

Exhaustible resources, common resources and pubic goods,
externalities.

Ch. 4

Flooding in England. Hurricane Mitch. BSE.

AUDIO AND TV

TV 02 – strong on diversity of interpretations of relationship
between natural and social – viewed through the example of disability.
Challenge to dominant models reflects some of health debate. Good
example of the value of qualitative evidence, personal narratives.

**What connections did you note between Block 2 and debates about the city, building
on our brainstorm at the start of Section 2.2?**

We noted:

- Evidence: Rogers piece does not display the rigour in use of evidence we
  explored in Block 2. Verifying and supporting his claims would need
  much more evidence, across more cities.

- Chapter 3 – key connection, helps explain patterns of linear city.

  Account of markets/externalities, public goods – helps explain why cities
  are linear/environmentally damaging.

- Chapter 4 – connection of the account of the risk society.

  Is it possible to argue that at the global level environmental risks derive
  from unsustainable linear cities?

- Chapter 2 – social model of health – could draw upon this to explain
  patterns of illness and mortality in cities.

NB: some issues in Block 2 have not been dealt with, i.e. role of biological
body/genetic structures.

Summary time! You should take the chance now to:

● Make sure you understand each of the points raised.

● Decide whether you disagree with any of them.

● Note any points of your own that we have missed or insufficiently developed, especially relevant links to Block 2.

SUMMARY

The city, and the natural and the social.

● The city should be thought about as a complex interaction of natural and social systems, and should not be diametrically opposed to a pure natural countryside.

● Cities are major sites of environmental problems both within the city and elsewhere, i.e. its ecological footprint.

● Environmental and social problems are closely intertwined.

● Some cities are more environmentally problematic than others, especially linear, sprawling, car- and market-driven cities.

2.3 The city, and order and power

What kinds of connections and relationships between the city and the key themes of Block 3 can you think of? How might we think about the relationships between the city and ordering, the city and power, the city and changing institutions? Jot down any notes or ideas you have.

Our brainstorm came up with this:

1 Cities can be sites of social order – think about the way in which transport systems, the physical infrastructure of cities etc. impose a pattern of movement, living, and working on its inhabitants (see Raban's 'Soft city' in Reading 1).

2 Cities can be sites of social disorder, confusion, uncertainty – identity crisis, fear of crime and violence, and ecological disruption (see Readings 1 and 2 on these points).

3 City planning and government can be thought of as institutions and discourses that attempt to create or impose order. Their transformation, delegitimization or fragmentation could also be a source of disorder – with variable consequences for different social groups.

ACTIVITY 5

Make notes on Reading 3.

As you read the extract, ask yourself:

- What visions of urban order does the reading describe?
- How is that order to be achieved? By what institutions, by the exercise of what kinds of power?
- How have post-war efforts and plans to create order changed?

READING 3

Allan Cochrane: 'Administered cities'

Building urban utopias

There has been a strong popular, as well as architectural and professional, tradition that links utopian visions of the future with attempts to plan urban development on a grand scale [...] Approaches which seek to remake cities in the image of planned utopias (however modest) have been subjected to increasingly harsh criticism in recent years. The most influential examples of such approaches, on which attention has frequently been focused, are those associated with **Ebenezer Howard** [...] and **Le Corbusier**. [...]

In some respects the approaches of these two writers look dramatically different. Howard aims for low density, while Le Corbusier celebrates high density. Howard's vision is of networks of relatively small garden cities linked into a social city; Le Corbusier starts from the vision of the central city and aims for a population of three million. Howard is looking for ways of bypassing the intensity of urban life; Le Corbusier is excited by it, but believes it can be managed. Although both emphasize the value of green space in the cities, Le Corbusier's approach creates that space by constructing high-rise buildings above the earth, alongside elevated roadways, while Howard incorporates green areas within his networks of settlements and in wedges which stretch into the heart of his cities. Commentators on these ideas have also been divided. Sennett (1990, p.171) notes that Le Corbusier dismisses Howard's vision for producing 'worthy, healthy, organic, and boring quasi-suburbs, dedicated to the proposition that coziness is life'. Hall (1996) dismisses Le Corbusier as 'an authoritarian centralist', arguing that Howard's vision, by contrast, was rooted in anarchist urban utopias of self-help in constructing the 'good city' [...] Howard's garden cities, stresses Hall, 'were merely the vehicles for a progressive reconstruction of capitalist society into an infinity of co-operative commonwealths' (p.87).

Others, however, have pointed to similarities, suggesting that both dismiss the messiness and inherent conflict of urban life and seek to replace them with sanitized alternatives. Both favoured starting with cleared or greenfield sites: Howard by using land outside existing cities, and Le Corbusier by levelling ground to create empty space on which to build. According to Jacobs (1961),

Ebenezer Howard

Liberal social reformer and founder of the Garden City movement, Howard argued for the creation of self-sustaining, planned small cities in rural areas. His ideas led to the creation of Letchworth (1903) and Welwyn Garden City (1920) which served as prototypes for Britain's post-war new towns.

Le Corbusier

Born Charles Edouard Janneret in 1887, Le Corbusier was a defining figure of modernist architecture and city planning, advocating a functional rationalism in design and with a taste for the sculptural qualities of rough cast concrete.

the rather different visions of Ebenezer Howard and Le Corbusier both remove the possibility of surprise and serve to undermine the possibility of organic development within cities, limiting the scope for social innovation. [...]

As Harvey points out, they appeared to share a belief that

> the proper design of *things* would solve all the problems in the social process. It was assumed that if you could just build your urban village, like Ebenezer Howard, or your Radiant City, like Le Corbusier, then the thing would have the power to keep the process forever in harmonious state.
>
> (Harvey, 1997, p.24)

Both Howard and Le Corbusier could be accused of seeking to solve (and indeed to define) what they saw as the social problems of the city in physical terms. [...] The answer for both of them was to change the layout of cities, to provide clearer and more logical forms of social segregation.

Although neither Howard nor Le Corbusier saw their own plans implemented on any scale, their approaches helped to influence the direction of state intervention in many urban areas by suggesting that the social problems of the slums might be overcome through forms of physical planning and spatial sorting. If there is any universal 'villain' identified by those writing on the management of urban space and urban development in recent years, it is Le Corbusier. That may seem strange for someone who saw only relatively few examples of his work – and none of his grand schemes – achieve built form. Neither the 'contemporary city' nor the 'radiant city' was every built. [...] Yet Le Corbusier's influence on a generation of planners and architects is taken for granted. His stress on 'killing' the street (by separating roads from pedestrians) and the clear hierarchies of function and style have been blamed for the more mundane and less ambitious plans for public housing and high-rise development that characterized much urban planning in the 1950s and 1960s. [...]

Nor does Howard escape from these critics. Sennett (1990, p.201) complains that 'Faced with the fact of social hostility in the city, the planner's impulse in the

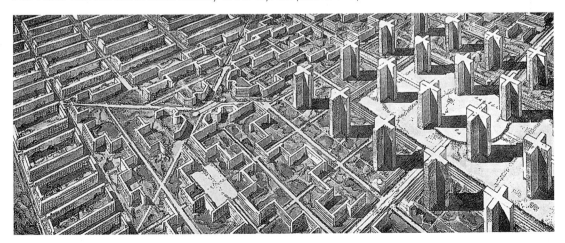

Le Corbusier's vision of the contemporary city

real world is to seal off conflicting or dissonant sides, to build internal walls rather than permeable borders'. He links this impulse back to the garden city movement, whose techniques, he argues, 'are now increasingly used in the city centre to remove the threat of classes or races touching, to create a city of secure inner walls'. [...] Instead of celebrating and building on networks of connection within cities, these models seek to maintain existing disconnections and impose new ones through forms of social as well as functional segregation: that is, separating housing from employment and green space from traffic. [...]

There is a real tension in the critiques that have been made of the utopian urbanists. On the one hand it is suggested that their aim was to remove conflict and tension and to sanitize and deaden urban life – to plan away the possibility of conflict to achieve the general de-intensification of urban life. [...] The role of the urban planners after 1945 has been criticized as an attempt to sanitize and to remove unevenness, when it is precisely the unevenness and variety that gives urban places their vitality. [...] Thus Donald (1997, p.200) criticizes Le Corbusier's vision of the radiant city for having 'the chill of Necropolis about it', and for 'Removing the organic and substituting the mechanical'. Jacobs (1961, p.386) claims that *a city cannot be a work of art ... To approach a city, or even a city neighbourhood, as if it were a larger architectural problem, capable of being given order by converting it into a disciplined work of art, is to make the mistake of attempting to substitute art for life*' (emphasis in original); and Rogers (1997, p.17) argues that 'such single-minded visions of cities are no longer relevant to the diversity and complexity of modern society'.

At the same time the utopians are criticized for the failure, not so much of their visions, but their inherent unattainability in practice. From this perspective, then, the problem is

- not so much that what they produce is sanitized, standardized and suburbanized (that is, removing uncertainty and fear),
- but rather that it produces spaces which are less protected and generate more violence and more fear.

Newman (1972, p.24), for example, is quite explicit in claiming that the legacy of Le Corbusier is the building of housing which does not provide 'defensible space' for its residents. 'Defensible space', according to Newman, is space in which 'latent territoriality and sense of community in the inhabitants can be translated into responsibility for ensuring a safe, productive, and well-maintained living space. The potential criminal perceives such a space as controlled by its residents, leaving him an intruder easily recognized and dealt with' (Newman, 1972, p.3). Such space, he argues, disappears in the enclosed vision of Le Corbusier and those pursuing his legacy, in part because of the density of settlement associated with them. [...]

It is all too easy just to dismiss the visions of the utopians and to conclude that the answer is simply to let everything just work itself out in some more or less organic or natural way. [...]

Even before Le Corbusier, there were dangerous places in cities, and there are dangerous places in cities which are so far relatively untouched by the power of urban planning and the orthogonal grid.

- The rejection of grand plans does not remove the problems of administration.

It merely forces us to rethink them. The rejection of any form of collective intervention implies a lack of popular control over development, but collective control does not mean that the development process ceases to generate inequality or to produce negative outcomes for some urban residents.

- Patterns of urban development reflect and express the relations of power that predominate in cities.

So, for example, the rejection of administration through state planning might also be consistent with a model of privatized control in which gated cities protect (and isolate) the overwhelmingly white middle classes from the poor, black [...]

The absence of state planning does not mean that there is no planning. For example, Houston in Texas has frequently been identified as an unplanned city – that is, one in which the market is left to determine the appropriate form of development with little in the way of formal intervention from state professionals, and little attempt to impose a plan from on high. As Sudjic notes, however,

> Houston, supposedly the most unplanned city of all, is in fact nothing of the kind. It is perfectly true that Houston has no zoning legislation, unlike almost every other major city in the United States. The voters of Houston rejected the idea as recently as 1962, but though they might change their minds one day, the city is certainly not without planning, and it has an armoury of regulations that achieve very much the same ends. What makes Houston – the Third Coast as it presumptuously calls itself – different is the extent to which development control is in the hands of the private landowners and developers who have made fortunes out of the city's explosive growth.

> Right up until the 1960s, Houston was run from regular meetings at a suite in the Lamar Hotel by a clique that made the decisions, formed the committees and fired the mayors. Taxes and services were kept at survival level, with infrastructure investment put off until crisis point was reached. They used tax money to bail out their flooded suburbs and to provide water and sewers for private developments ...

(Sudjic, 1992, p.97)

The recognition that planning is not simply a 'rational' or a technical process, but is rather one of negotiation, argument and accommodation, opens up other possibilities for conceiving ways of managing, or administering, urban development. [...] Order cannot simply be imposed. Instead it must be recognized that the world of urban politics is made up of a series of negotiations and partnerships, linking a range of social actors, which might include elected governments and their professional staffs, non-elected statutory institutions, non-statutory and private sector agencies of various sorts, as well as communities, groups and individual citizens. [...]

The term 'governance' is increasingly preferred to 'government' to capture both the potential complexity of these relationships and to indicate that some more or less stable or accepted set of arrangements may arise from them, at least for significant lengths of time. In other words, just because there is a high degree of complexity, the rules, practices and political structures of urban living may still operate to maintain order in an apparently 'unruly' urban world. [...]

At the heart of the debates about urban administration and governance is a tension between attempts to achieve fixity and to work or manage fluidity. In practice, the dominant approaches have tended to search for ways of capturing the social relations of cities in more or less unitary models of development and governance. [...] 'perhaps what are needed are active democratic processes for defining the public good, recognizing the conflicts over it, and allowing it to change over time'.

According to one powerful history of the governance of urban change, since the 1970s there has been a dramatic shift in approach away from models that seek to develop a coherent and holistic system of social and economic planning. This has increasingly been dismissed as undesirable as well as unfeasible. Not only, it is argued, are such approaches unable to cope with the complexity and diversity of human society, but they are likely to impose unacceptable controls on those whose lives they seek to manage or improve. Instead, it is argued, it has become necessary to focus on what makes cities successful as living environments [...]

Stress is placed on the need to move away from attempts to produce detailed master plans of urban development within which everybody has to fit, towards approaches that reflect a more organic understanding of the nature of urban development and aim at allowing (defending or creating) space in which a plurality of citizen and community voices may be heard. Instead of attempting to capture or fix social relations through the formal rules of urban living or the design of buildings, it is suggested that approaches to urban governance and urban development should concentrate on identifying and celebrating the possibilities of flexibility and fluidity. [...]

One response to concerns about the exclusion of urban residents from popular decision-making might simply be to argue for (improved) traditional representative democratic arrangements as a means of ensuring involvement in debates about urban development and the running of cities. Such arrangements generally involve the election of local councils which oversee the operation of professionals of one sort or another in the delivery of services and the operation of planning. Unfortunately, this model has itself been challenged substantially in recent years, both because its record of responsiveness and involvement has not always been impressive, and because it implies a standardized approach to an increasingly diversified set of issues [...] The notion of citizen that underlies the traditional western model of local democracy is a curiously passive one, in which representatives are elected to oversee the work of others, with little expectation of further involvement by electors in decision-making.

Attempts have been made, however, to identify other ways of approaching these issues. Hirst (1994) [...] for example, [has] highlighted the possibilities of [...] 'associative democracy'. This builds on the notion that society is made up of a plurality of associations, through which individuals come together in a complex variety of ways reflecting their multiple identities (at work, in leisure, at home, as consumer, and so on). In other words, it starts from assumptions about heterogeneity and difference, rather than homogeneity. It rejects the notion of 'community' as a homogeneous basis for political activity. Although these associations are not necessarily urban, many of them are based in cities and come together in ways which help to define them in terms that recognize the importance of local diversity, and differences between places as well as between groups and individuals. [...]

Hirst [argues] that instead of trying to find some overall (planning) logic to which everyone then needs to conform, it would be better to allow these groups to develop their own agendas and to implement them.

This is consistent with the arguments developed by Jane Jacobs (1961, p.16), who says that 'Cities are an immense laboratory of trial and error, failure and success, in city building and city design. This is the laboratory in which city planning should have been learning and forming and testing its theories'. 'Most city diversity', she argues, 'is the creation of incredible numbers of different people and different private organizations, with vastly differing ideas and purposes, planning outside the formal framework of public action' (Jacobs, 1961, p.256). Jacobs argues that what is needed is the prospect of gradually building from small-scale successes to a renewed urban vision, based on a carefully managed mix of uses and populations at street, neighbourhood and district level.

Jacobs' approach also highlights some of the problems with notions of associative democracy. Her emphasis on 'community-based' self-help and informal relations is based on an overwhelmingly positive view of social relations in cities, and the networks of relations she describes generate a positive spiral of social interaction and security. However, her rosy view of urban neighbourhoods fails to take into account some of the pressures of city life and, in particular, the concentration of populations with marginal economic positions whose members are excluded from employment or trapped in casualized sectors of employment. [...]

The power relations expressed in the socio-spatial patterning of cities makes some of the more optimistic hopes of 'associative democracy' look less convincing, because access to membership of the different associations is unlikely to be equal.

Who determines which people are allowed to join which groups? How can powerful agencies (such as major developers) be controlled? How, as Amin and Thrift (1995) ask, can differences between localities be resolved?

References

Amin, A. and Thrift, N. (1995) 'Institutional issues for the European regions: from markets and plans to socioeconomics and powers of association', *Economy and Society*, vol.24, pp.41–66.

Donald, J. (1997) 'This, here, now: imagining the modern city', in Westwood, S. and Williams, J. (eds) *Imagining Cities: Scripts, Signs, Memory*, London, Routledge.

Hall, P. (1996) *Cities of Tomorrow: An Intellectual History of Urban Planning and Design in the Twentieth Century*, Oxford, Blackwell.

Harvey, D. (1997) 'Contested cities: social process and spatial form', in Jewson, N. and MacGregor, S. (eds) *Transforming Cities: Contested Governance and New Spatial Divisions*, London, Routledge.

Hirst, P. (1994) *Associative Democracy: New Forms of Economic and Social Governance*, Cambridge, Polity Press.

Jacobs, J. (1961) *The Death and Life of Great American Cities*, quotes from 1964 edn, Harmondsworth, Penguin.

Newman, O. (1972) *Defensible Space: People and Design in the Violent City*, London, Architectural Press.

Rogers, R. (1997) *Cities for a Small Planet*, edited by Philip Gumuchdjian, London, Faber and Faber.

Sennett, R. (1990) *The Conscience of the Eye: The Design and Social Life in Cities*, London, Faber and Faber.

Sudjic, D. (1992) *The 100 Mile City*, San Diego, Harcourt, Brace and Company.

Source: Cochrane, 1999, pp.310–19, 328–30

C O M M E N T

Our notes looked like this:

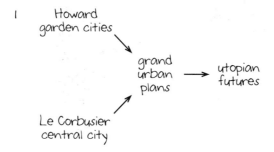

1   Howard
     garden cities

          grand
          urban ⟶ utopian
          plans   futures

     Le Corbusier
     central city

2   Visions of cities

Howard	Le Corbusier
Low density	High density
Periphery more important than centre	Centre dominates periphery
Bypass city intensity	Excited by intensity
Criticized for cosiness	Criticized as authoritarian centralist

3 But both criticized for sanitizing cities, eroding diversity/
   messiness and assuming plan and design is dominant/key force
   for change.

4 Impact of both models on post-war city considerable but
   complex:

   Le Corbusier → Mundane public housing, car domination.

   Howard →   Encourage segregation and division of
                    cities by class and ethnicity.

   Grand plans →   Failure to create defensible space
                    (NB connections to Introductory
                    Block/crime.

5 But rejection of grand plans:
   (a) Still leaves problem of administration.
   (b) And admin/planning is always enmeshed in city's structure of
       power.
   (c) Absence of planning leaves order in hands of private sector,
       e.g. Houston.

6 So if planning is about negotiation and politics, what models of
   urban governance are there?

   Post-1970s – shift from grand plans to plural/diverse/organic
   governance.

   Options:
   (a) Local representative democracy – but has limits.
   (b) Hirst's associative democracy – but still problems of unequal
       power of associations.
   (c) Jacobs – bottom-up, small-scale, multi-sector trial and
       error.

Combining these notes with our earlier brainstorm, we drew Diagram D.

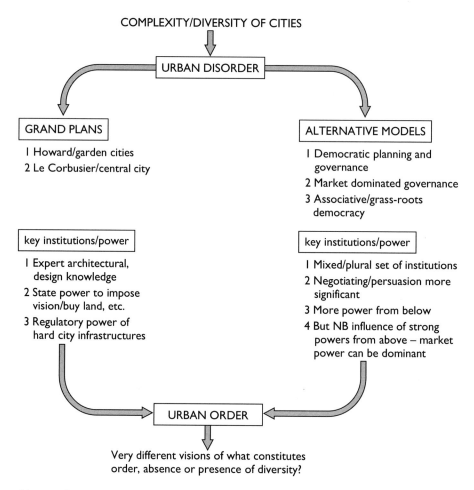

Diagram D

As you can probably see, there are plenty of connections between these debates and those that you looked at in Block 3. The same kinds of arguments were addressed but with regard to other institutions and other forms of order, such as families, work, and welfare. So now is the time to go back to Block 3.

ACTIVITY 6

Look back over your notes on Block 3. If you have not collected them together or reduced them, take the opportunity now to have a go. We are going to work with the same set of questions as we did in Section 2.1, Activity 2.

● What were the key questions of the block?

● In what ways were the course themes used?

● In what ways did each chapter in the block address these issues? What were the key debates in each chapter?

- What were the key case studies, the best examples, and the types of empirical evidence used?

- What additional materials from the audio-cassette and the TV programme can you use?

C O M M E N T

Our quick notes looked like this:

QUESTIONS

1 How do social institutions order lives?

2 How does power work in and through social institutions to order lives?

3 How have political ideologies influenced changes in power and ordering?

THEMES

U+D

Are changes in social institutions and their ordering producing uncertainty? Are the characteristics of family life, working life and the welfare state creating uncertainty? Why?

Is there an increasing diversity to the institutions of work, welfare and the family?

Is this a source of uncertainty? Is it a source of liberation, increasing choice? For whom?

S+A

Social institutions operate as structures both constraining agency and providing opportunities for agency.

The structure of institutions helps determine who is empowered and who is constrained by those structures.

Key link – all structures create and distribute power – in its many forms.

K+K

Narrative. Shifting fortunes and strengths of political ideologies have helped initiate, support and legitimize structural changes in family life, work and welfare provision. Knowledge in general and political ideologies in particular are sources of social power.

Analytical. Explores how claims and concepts combine to generate theories that can do explanatory work. Looks at how theories are shaped by the moral/normative values they embrace and how theories shape what kinds of evidence one draws upon and how that evidence is interpreted.

CHAPTERS AND DEBATES

Ch. 1

Develops vocabulary for describing power - persuasion, coercion, domination, etc.

Offers two models of theorizing power - Weber vs. Foucault, power from above and below.

Offers explanations of expert authority and power (see Block 5 on experts).

Tests theories of power in connection with call centre.

Ch. 2

Account of family change - explores character of diversity and link to uncertainty.

Contrasts feminist and conservative accounts of change and its consequences.

Note different moral perspectives of these ideologies shapes theoretical argument.

Ch. 3

Account of shift in labour market from security to insecurity, inflexibility to flexibility.

Compares liberal and social democratic accounts of labour markets and connection to macroeconomic issues.

Ch. 4

Account of shift in welfare state from 'golden age' of security to insecurity - but argues that contrast exaggerated.

EVIDENCE AND EXAMPLES

Ch. 1

GM foods debate on modes of power, role of experts. Call centres to explore Weber vs. Foucault and use of theory.

Ch. 2

Quantitative data on shifting structure of family life.

Ch. 3

Quantitative data on flexibility in labour market gender differences.

Case study of Rover to illuminate role of power in changing labour market.

Ch. 4

Transformation of welfare state under Conservatives, 1979-97, as case study for exploring restructuring of institutions, role of social values and ideologies in shaping change.

AUDIO AND TV

TV 03 – qualitative evidence through diversity of personal biographies of generational shift in attitude to security, identity and work. Anecdotal evidence of diversity of change in the labour market and the structural creation of both insecurity and opportunity.

What connections did you note between Block 3 and the material in this section on the city, order and power?

We noted:

1   That the relationship between cities, order and disorder is not dissimilar to the relationship between the key institutions of Block 3 and order and disorder. It may be that these parallel narratives are intertwined – a disorderly labour market and welfare state help create urban disorder.

2   That in all these cases diversity can be seen as a source of disorder and uncertainty. That narrative accounts of institutional change are all prone to over-romanticizing the past, and unnecessarily denigrating the present (see Section 3.1 of this review).

3   That the two models of power – Weber's and Foucault's – are applicable to the different models of urban planning.
    Weberian: top-down, grand plans.
    Foucault: diffuse, fluid and changing plans.

4   That critiques of social-democratic planning in the welfare state (Marxist, feminists, liberals) can be applied to urban grand designs.

5   Each approach attempts to create its preferred version of social order.

Summary time! You can take the chance now to:

- Make sure you understand each of the points raised.

- Decide whether you disagree with any of them.

- Note any points of your own that we have missed or insufficiently developed, especially relevant links to Block 3.

SUMMARY

The city, and order and power.

- Cities are sites of both social order and disorder, linked to and shaping other patterns and institutions of social order, e.g. families/ work.

- Cities' diversity and messiness tends towards social disorder.

- Urban planning and governance is a response to that disorder – like political programmes for reinventing families or regulating labour markets.

- Grand designs for urban planning all share a top-down approach to power and policy, eradicating or containing infrastructural and social diversity. These have foundered on the intractable *diversity and instability* of cities.

- Alternative models of governance see power produced and used by multiple agents competing in markets, and collaborating in networks and negotiations.

- However, these models rarely take into account the enormous differences in power of different urban actors, groups, etc.

2.4 The city and globalization

What kinds of connections and relationships between the city and globalization can you think of? Don't confine yourself to just the issues raised in Block 4. There may be connections with earlier material in the course. Jot down any notes or ideas you have.

From our quick mental reviews of Blocks 1–3 we noted:

- The ethnic make-up of urban populations must be closely related to patterns of global migration.

- A city's ecological footprint may have a global reach. Cities in turn are affected by global environmental problems.

- The structure of employment in cities may be related to the impact of the global economy on a city's economy.

We will explore these kinds of connections in more detail below, but first let's try and summarize the content of Block 4. As you do so, try and think about any connections you might make to the experience of cities.

ACTIVITY 7

Look back over your notes on Block 4. If you have not collected them together or reduced them, take the opportunity now to have a go. We are going to work with the same set of questions as we did in Section 2.1, Activity 2.

- What were the key questions of the block?

- In what ways were the course themes used?

- In what ways did each chapter in the block address these issues? What were the key debates in each chapter?

- What were the key case studies, the best examples, and the types of empirical evidence used?

- What additional materials from the audio-cassettes and the TV programme can you use?

C O M M E N T

Our quick notes looked like this:

QUESTIONS

1 What is globalization? How best conceived?

2 How significant is contemporary globalization? Historical comparisons?

3 Impact of globalization on autonomy and sovereignty of nation-state?

4 Winners and losers?

THEMES

U+D

Uncertainty — old order of sovereign nation-sates and Westphalian international order undermined by globalization — uncertainty about role, power and legitimacy of nation-states, international organizations, etc.

Diversity — cultural globalization force for national diversity — can also be seen as diminishing diversity through Americanization.

S+A

Globalization creates new global structures (political, cultural, economic) which shape/constrain agency of individuals, nation-states, etc.

All structures have spatial dimension – global, regional, national, local.

Globalization produces new agents – international NGOs and alliances, international organizations.

K+K

Narrative – cultural globalization force for spreading diversity of information to many, can undermine elite and expert knowledge.

Analytical – introduces skill of evaluating theories and claims – through criteria of coherence, empirical adequacy, comprehensiveness.

CHAPTERS AND DEBATES

Ch. 1

Strong on models of globalization and vocabulary/ conceptualization for describing global networks – globalists vs. traditionalists vs. transformationalists.

Ch. 2

Presents globalists, traditionalists and transformationalists on impact of cultural globalization.

Notes interconnection of these positions with political ideologies (esp. in Workbook 4, Sect. 2).

Ch. 3

Presents strong traditionalist case on economic globalization. Explores origins of winners and losers economically.

Ch. 4

Strong transformationalist position. Explores some globalist and traditionalist critiques, esp. in Workbook 4, Sect. 4. Contrasts contemporary international order with old Westphalian system. Explores origins of uncertainty. Possibility of re-regulating globalization.

EVIDENCE AND EXAMPLES

Ch. 1

Draws up models of globalization through interconnectedness, infrastructure, etc. and explores types of evidence that would build on this.

Mapping globalization.

Good case study of environmental globalization.

Ch. 2

Strong use of quantitative data on TV exports and viewing.

Qualitative evidence on how TV is received and read by viewers.

Case study of telegraph vs. the Internet.

Ch. 3

Strong use of quantitative data on trade and overseas investment to explore contemporary globalization and make historical comparisons.

Ch. 4

Case studies main form of evidence – esp. MAI protest, regulating the drug trade. The East Asian financial crisis

AUDIO AND TV

Giddens' lecture and conversation (Audio-cassette 7, Sides A and B) good example of globalist-transformationalist arguments.

TV 04 – enriches the account of cultural globalization, interesting material on technological determinism, Japan case study good contrasts with UK focus of the book.

So how does this material connect to the fate of cities in the post-war UK? Looking over our notes we wondered whether we could connect the different forms of globalization dealt with in Chapters 2–4 to different aspects of city life.

We came up with Diagram E.

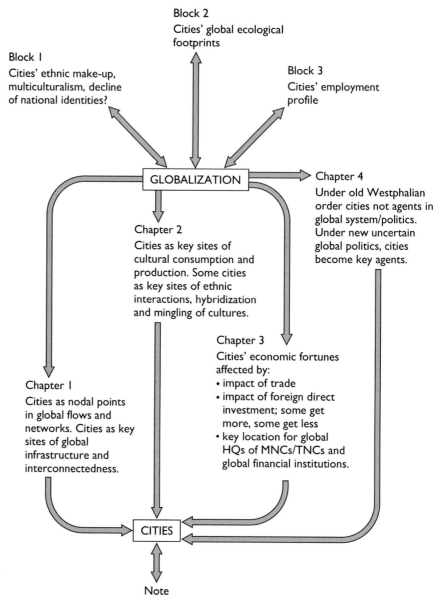

Block 2
Cities' global ecological footprints

Block 1
Cities' ethnic make-up, multiculturalism, decline of national identities?

Block 3
Cities' employment profile

GLOBALIZATION

Chapter 4
Under old Westphalian order cities not agents in global system/politics. Under new uncertain global politics, cities become key agents.

Chapter 2
Cities as key sites of cultural consumption and production. Some cities as key sites of ethnic interactions, hybridization and mingling of cultures.

Chapter 3
Cities' economic fortunes affected by:
• impact of trade
• impact of foreign direct investment; some get more, some get less
• key location for global HQs of MNCs/TNCs and global financial institutions.

Chapter 1
Cities as nodal points in global flows and networks. Cities as key sites of global infrastructure and interconnectedness.

CITIES

Note
• Fate of cities very <u>diverse</u>, global impacts vary locally. Some cities are winners, some losers.
• Different perspectives on globalization will give different accounts of the role and fate of the city.

Diagram E

ACTIVITY 8

Now let's try and develop some of these arguments a bit further.

Make short notes on the following readings.

As you read them consider:

- What is the relative weight in the two readings of global and local forces/structures?

- Which, if any, of the three models of globalization developed in Block 4 do the authors appear to be deploying?

- In what way do the readings inform our understanding of globalization's winners and losers?

- To what extent are issues of *uncertainty and diversity* and *structure and agency* raised within the extracts? What structures? What agents?

Saskia Sassen: 'The global city'

The point of departure for the present study is that the combination of spatial dispersal and global integration has created a new strategic role for major cities. Beyond their long history as centers for international trade and banking, these cities now function in four new ways: first, as highly concentrated command points in the organization of the world economy; second, as key locations for finance and for specialized service firms, which have replaced manufacturing as the leading economic sectors; third, as sites of production, including the production of innovations, in these leading industries; and fourth, as markets for the products and innovations produced. These changes in the functioning of cities have had a massive impact upon both international economic activity and urban form: cities concentrate control over vast resources, while finance and specialized service industries have restructured the urban social and economic order. Thus a new type of city has appeared. It is the global city. Leading examples now are New York, London, and Tokyo. [...]

As I shall show, these three cities have undergone massive and *parallel* changes in their economic base, spatial organization, and social structure. But this parallel development is a puzzle. How could cities with as diverse a history, culture, politics, and economy as New York, London and Tokyo experience similar transformations concentrated in so brief a period of time? [...]

How does the position of these cities in the world economy today differ from that which they have historically held as centers of banking and trade? When Max Weber analyzed the medieval cities woven together in the Hanseatic League, he conceived their trade as the exchange of surplus production; it was his view that a medieval city could withdraw from external trade and continue to support itself, albeit on a reduced scale. The modern molecule of global cities is nothing like the trade among self-sufficient places in the Hanseatic League, as Weber understood it. The first thesis advanced in this book is that the territorial dispersal of current economic activity creates a need for expanded central control and management. In other words, while in principle the territorial decentralization of economic activity in recent years could have been accompanied by a corresponding decentralization in ownership and hence in the appropriation of profits, there has been little movement in that direction. Though large firms have increased their subcontracting to smaller firms, and many national firms in the newly industrializing countries have grown rapidly, this form of growth is ultimately part of a chain. Even industrial homeworkers in remote rural areas are now part of that chain. The transnational corporations continue to control much of the end product and to reap the profits associated with selling in the world market. The internationalization and expansion of the financial industry has brought growth to a large number of smaller financial markets, a growth which has fed the expansion of the global industry. But top-level control and management of the industry has become concentrated in a few leading financial centers, notably New York, London, and Tokyo. These account for a disproportionate share of all financial transactions and one that has grown rapidly since the early 1980s. The fundamental dynamic posited here is that the more globalized the economy becomes, the higher the agglomeration of central functions in a relatively few sites, that is, the global cities.

The extremely high densities evident in the business districts of these cities are one spatial expression of this logic. The widely accepted notion that density and agglomeration will become obsolete because global telecommunications advances allow for maximum population and resource dispersal is poorly conceived. It is, I argue, precisely because of the territorial dispersal facilitated by telecommunication that agglomeration of certain centralizing activities has sharply increased. [...]

A second major theme of this chapter concerns the impact of this type of economic growth on the economic order within these cities. [...] Global cities are [...] sites for (1) the production of specialized services needed by complex organizations for running a spatially dispersed network of factories, offices, and service outlets; and (2) the production of financial innovations and the making of markets, both central to the internationalization and expansion of the financial industry. [...]

A key dynamic running through these various activities and organizing my analysis of the place of global cities in the world economy is their capability for producing global control. By focusing on the production of services and financial innovations, I am seeking to displace the focus of attention from the familiar issues of the power of large corporations over governments and economies, or supercorporate concentration of power through interlocking directorates or organizations, such as the IMF. I want to focus on an aspect that has received less attention, which could be referred to as the 'practice' of global control: the work of producing and reproducing the organization and management of a global production system and a global marketplace for finance. [...]

A third major theme [is] the consequences of these developments for the national urban system in each of these countries and for the relationship of the global city to its nation-state. While a few major cities are the sites of production for the new global control capability, a large number of other major cities have lost their role as leading export centers for industrial manufacturing, as a result of the decentralization of this form of production. Cities such as Detroit, Liverpool, Manchester, and now increasingly Nagoya and Osaka have been affected by the decentralization of their key industries at the domestic and international levels. According to the first hypothesis presented above, this same process has contributed to the growth of service industries that produce the specialized inputs to run global production processes and global markets for inputs and outputs. These industries – international legal and accounting services, management consulting, financial services – are heavily concentrated in cities such as New York, London, and Tokyo. We need to know how this growth alters the relations between the global cities and what were once the leading industrial centers in their nations. Does globalization bring about a triangulation so that New York, for example, now plays a role in the fortunes of Detroit that it did not play when that city was home to one of the leading industries, auto manufacturing? Or, in the case of Japan, we need to ask, for example, if there is a connection between the increasing shift of production out of Toyota City (Nagoya) to offshore locations (Thailand, South Korea, and the United States) and the development for the first time of a new headquarters for Toyota in Tokyo. [...]

The new international forms of economic activity raise a problem about the relationship between nation-states and global cities. [...] I posit the possibility of systematic discontinuity between what used to be thought of as national growth and the forms of growth evident in global cities in the 1980s. These cities constitute a system rather than merely competing with each other. What contributes to growth in the network of global cities may well not contribute to growth in nations. [...]

The fourth and final theme [...] concerns the impact of these new forms of and conditions for growth on the social order of the global city. There is a vast body of literature on the impact of a dynamic, high-growth manufacturing sector in the highly developed countries, which shows that it raised wages, reduced inequality, and contributed to the formation of a middle class. Much less is known about the sociology of a service economy. Daniel Bell's (1973) *The Coming of Post-Industrial Society* posits that such an economy will result in growth in the number of highly educated workers and a more rational relation of workers to issues of social equity. [...]

Major growth industries show a greater incidence of jobs in the high- and low-paying ends of the scale than do the older industries now in decline. Almost half the jobs in the producer services are lower-income jobs, and half are in the two highest earnings classes. In contrast, a large share of manufacturing workers were in the middle-earning jobs during the postwar period of high growth in these industries in the United States and United Kingdom.

Two other developments in global cities have also contributed to economic polarization. One is the vast supply of low-wage jobs required by high-income gentrification in both its residential and commercial settings. The increase in the numbers of expensive restaurants, luxury housing, luxury hotels, gourmet shops, boutiques, French hand laundries, and special cleaners that ornament the new urban landscape illustrates this trend. Furthermore, there is a continuing need for low-wage industrial services, even in such sectors as finance and specialized services. A second development that has reached significant proportions is what I call the downgrading of the manufacturing sector, a process in which the share of unionized shops declines and wages deteriorate while sweatshops and industrial homework proliferate. This process includes the downgrading of jobs within existing industries and the job supply patterns of some of the new industries, notably electronics assembly. It is worth noting that the growth of a downgraded manufacturing sector has been strongest in cities such as New York and London.

The expansion of low-wage jobs as a function of *growth* trends implies a reorganization of the capital–labor relation. To see this, it is important to distinguish the characteristics of jobs from their sectoral location, since highly dynamic, technologically advanced growth sectors may well contain low-wage dead-end jobs. Furthermore, the distinction between sectoral characteristics and sectoral growth patterns is crucial: backward sectors, such as downgraded manufacturing or low-wage service occupations, can be part of major growth trends in a highly developed economy. It is often assumed that backward sectors express decline trends. Similarly, there is a tendency to assume that advanced sectors, such as finance, have mostly good, white-collar jobs. In fact, they contain a good number of low-paying jobs, from cleaner to stock clerk.

Reference

Bell, D. (1973) *The Coming of Post-Industrial Society: A Venture in Social Forecasting*, New York, Basic Books

Source: Sassen, 1991/1996, pp.61–8

READING 5

Ian Taylor: 'Two tales of two cities'

Thinking about cities has been profoundly influenced by what the American researchers John Logan and Harvey Molotch referred to in the 1980s as, 'urban growth coalitions' – partnerships of senior private and public sector professionals working in architecture, transport and urban planning in close, frequently commercial relationships with developers. Their claim to speak on behalf of local urban populations in general has found increasing support over the last ten to fifteen years.[1] In the perspectives of these local growth coalitions, the challenge to all cities, especially old industrial cities in post-Fordist North America and Europe, was that of occupying a new niche in the image market – whether as a City of Sport, City of Drama, a City of Shopping or a Garden City. Meanwhile, large and ambitious cities, have preferred to identify themselves as 'headquarter cities' based on the new cultural, communication and financial industries. Logan and Molotch advance a taxonomy in which all post-industrial cities are seen to be launched into one of five redevelopment categories: in a few instances, as headquarter cities; more frequently as specialist module production cities which try to survive on the inherited skills of a local labour force; as border/entrepôt cities – primarily trading or commercial centres; as centres of sports and entertainment; or finally, as retirement cities.

This abstract typology of 'urban fortune' offers a starting point, but my own study of two North of England cities,[2] has suggested the understanding of urban futures may involve more detailed exploration of local and often very long-standing variation.

Between 1991 and 1994, our research into Manchester and Sheffield – two old industrial cities settled and built up during the middle years of the nineteenth century and seen as substantially similar 'old North of England cities' – unearthed the overwhelming sense of difference, not least in popular discussions of local urban futures.[3] In Greater Manchester – the site of two Olympic Game bids, City of Drama in 1994, home to the new Metrolink urban transit system, and, thanks in part to City Pride and other European monies, the centre of a considerable amount of new-build architecture – we encountered a widespread sense of being on the pioneering edge of urban change. The conurbation was perceived as a city with a job market capable of supporting some kind of economic future, but also one with a vibrant range of life-style attributes, especially for the young. In Sheffield, by contrast – a city which as recently as the early 1980s still thought of itself as the City of Steel, despite losing over 35,000 jobs in that industry in a very short time – the general mood was quite different. The initiatives taken – almost in panic, on some accounts – by the local council in the 1980s to deal with the unfolding economic catastrophe (most notably, their investment in the World Student Games in the failed attempt to reposition Sheffield as a national City of Sport) were widely criticised by local people, as was the Council's new South Yorkshire Supertram, which is far less successful than the Manchester Metrolink (which has vastly exceeded its own profit projections). Sheffielders also opined at length on the troubled condition of the city's shopping centre, which has been decimated by competition from the Meadowhall development on the city's East End, and the decline in the quality of life in the city – usually referenced in terms of the demise of the city bus system, consequent on government intervention with the city's famous Cheap Bus Fares policy of the 1970s and subsequent deregulation of local bus services. Other locals spoke with feeling of the steep increases reported in local crime rates. This in a city which has prided itself for many years as having one of the lowest crime levels of any major industrial city.

It's tempting to see this marked difference in local feeling as a specific product of recent economic developments, a demonstration of the mood shift that the dynamism of local, far-sighted enterprise can make. But in the discussions we held, another perspective was inescapable. For a great many Mancunians, the rapid changes occurring in their city are an expression of a long-established local character – notably, as home to the cotton industry's birth and rapid growth in the late eighteenth and early nineteenth century, working hard to market the products of its commercial activities as they spread across the region. The 'cottonopolis' connections to the wider world had been assured by the opening of the Manchester Ship Canal: by the 1840s, Manchester, the 'Shock City', was at the very centre of the whole Industrial Revolution. Later in the nineteenth century, as captains of this trade, the 'men who made Manchester' invested heavily, providing a material infrastructure of buildings and streets – the core of Victorian Manchester – and it was in this central area that the theatres, shopping arcades, schools of music and art galleries of Manchester quickly developed. 'What Manchester does today (in commercial or cultural terms)', went the saying, 'London (or the world) will do tomorrow.'

It is very difficult to escape the feeling that some very similar process has been applied to Manchester during the 1980s and 1990s. Not only are many of the new urban development initiatives driven by close networks of confident young or middle-aged Mancunian men, but there is also evidence of a fast developing local alternative economy of work and employment, based on a similar entrepreneurial or opportunistic common sense to that which nurtured the local economy at the height of the previous free trade movement. The organic connection between the local Manchester scally of that period and the street-wise 'Manc' of the 1990s is unmistakable. So too is the gendered character of both the urban leaderships and street-level economy – it seems primarily, once again, to be men who are remaking Manchester.

The cultural contrast with Sheffield is marked. There are some local examples of individual and corporate enterprise, not least in some key city centre locales such as the Tudor Square piazza, but urban change has mostly taken the form of the refurbishment of what is old and familiar rather than radical post modernist transformation. Cultural activity in the city seems very often preoccupied with the so recently lost world of the economy of cutlery and steel – for example, in the flourishing interest in local, industrial history and in dramas at the Crucible Theatre. Even the television advertising for William Stones' Sheffield Bitter relies on sepia images of the grafting steelworker, self-evidently having earned his pint reward.[4] A very large proportion of the discussions of 'global change and everyday life' in our Sheffield focus groups consisted of references to the past.

A purely economic analysis of residents' responses to the prospective futures of their cities would explain little. For all that Sheffield's labour market has in effect collapsed, and for all the other problems which residents of that city reported to us at great length, they do not appear very keen to leave. The total loss of population in the whole South Yorkshire area between 1981 and 1991 was only 47,900 people, or 0.4 per cent; of these, 33,900 were lost from the city of Sheffield (6.0 per cent of the population of 1981).[5] The contrast with the emigration from Merseyside in the 1970s and 1980s, and with the Northumberland and Durham coalfields over an even longer period, is striking. Our talks revealed a range of compensations for many people in living in the city – calculations which were always set against the poor economic prospects. These ranged from an appreciation of the city's physical location (ten minutes from open country), its celebrated system of parks and The Round Walk to other, more nebulous but powerfully-voiced characteristics such as its friendliness. These qualities have been the subject of comment for many years, attributed by some to its geographical location or that it is 'built around seven hills', and by others to the peculiar character of the cutlery and steel trade culture. The city has been seen as an 'enclave culture', originating around the workshop (the cutlery mill), the pub, the chapel and the private house, but with a longstanding sense of autonomy from wider England.

This comparative project into the local impacts of global change cautions against the generalising emphasis of so much contemporary urban analysis [...] My concern is not to deny the universal impact of global developments (on culture, economics or forms of political and urban representation), but to highlight the significance of 'residual' aspects of local culture. In one interview in Sheffield, for example, the activist leader of the Don Valley Forum wanted to see the 'dead space' around the central inner city reclaimed for use by market gardeners in the form of allotments, with space on higher ground for pigeon-racers. In Manchester, the home of the new national cycling Velodrome, many locals want to see a redesign of central city streets for cyclists, an impossible dream around the hills of Sheffield. Recent migrants into Manchester from Hong Kong want more viewing areas at Manchester International Airport to facilitate their Sunday hobby of watching international flights arriving and departing. Residents of the suburban areas of both cities were bent on improving their own neighbourhoods, nearly always in reference to reclaiming something of its specific local or village like character. These are the forms of 'local knowledge' on which innovative public and private sector urban development projects in Britain, closely attentive to local cultural differences in this old society, and sceptical of the universalising voice of the postmodernists, could depend.

Footnotes

1. Logan, J.R. and Harvey, L., 1987, *Urban fortunes: the political economy of place*, University of Chicago Press, Chicago.

2. Taylor, I., Evans, K. and Fraser, P., 1996, *A tale of two cities: global change, local feeling and everyday life in the North of England*, Routledge, London.

3. This research involved over thirty focus groups which brought together many different elements of the local public.

4. Given the closure of all the main steel plants in Sheffield during the 1980s, the sequence for these Sheffield Bitter adverts had actually to be filmed in Czechoslovakia. In 1995, only 4,500 people in Sheffield were employed in steel (compared to some 45,000 in 1971).

5. *County Report, South Yorkshire Part 1*, Table B, 1991 Census.

Source: Taylor, 1996, pp.22–4

COMMENT

Our short notes looked like this:

SASSEN – GLOBAL CITY

Spatial dispersal and global integration of economic activity → Key functions of global cities.

1. Demand for command points in a globalizing economy.

   Fragmentation and globalization of industry (transnational corporations with massive complex supply, production chains) creates need/demand for very concentrated centres of finance, control. New telecommunications facilitate this.

2. Concentration of new firms/industries.

   Therefore there is a growth of finance and service firms which concentrate in global cities making specialized services, control outputs and new financial instruments.

3. These cities thus become the site of new financial markets.

Combined, these factors restructure the urban order.

Some cities, especially manufacturing dependent cities, lose out, shrink.

Others become global cities, i.e. New York, Tokyo, London.

Patterns, rates of growth become detached from national growth/economy. Competition occurs between global cities rather than between nation-states.

Experience economic polarization as middle-pay jobs in manufacturing decline and new industries create jobs at high and low end of the pay scales.

Consumption patterns of new rich generate lots of low-paid service jobs.

What is left of manufacturing becomes low pay – downgraded manufacturing.

TAYLOR – TWO CITIES

Challenge for post-industrial cities – how to reinvent themselves. Options include: HQ city, specialist production, trading, sports/entertainment, retirement. (Logan and Molotch.)

Reinvention led by urban growth coalitions.

Taylor – research on Manchester and Sheffield – more focus needed on local particularities.

Manchester – successful, confident.

Sheffield – uncertain. NB panic/failure of sports bids.

Why difference, as global economic conditions on both similar?

Man. – draw on inherited identities and experience of great 19th C. commercial, cosmopolitan city.

Shef. – emphasis on preservation of lost past not reinvention, roots in idea of Sheffield as autonomous, enclave culture.

ACTIVITY 9

Now, drawing these notes together in terms of the questions posed at the start of Activity 8 we drew a grid.

Have a go at filling this in yourself and check it with our version at the end of this review on p.156.

Cities and globalization

	Sassen	Taylor
Global vs. local		
Models of globalization		

	Sassen	Taylor
Winners and losers		
Uncertainty and diversity		
Structures		
Agency		

Now look back to Diagram E (p.46).

How do our notes of Readings 4 and 5 enrich our initial account of the city and globalization?

We noted this:

- Sassen's model of the global city is an excellent example of the node and flow model of globalization outlined in Book 4, Chapter 1 that incorporates an understanding of the very localized power that key nodes/cities have over networks, especially economic networks.

- Sassen's account of cities and the global economy provides a *globalist* counterpoint to the more *traditionalist* account of economic globalization in Book 4, Chapter 3.

- Her detailed accounts of the transformation/social polarization of global cities draws together Block 1 on class, the city and globalization, but the account is very restricted. *Only* three cities. Only one UK city – London.

- Taylor's work provides us with a greater range of cities, illuminating their *diversity*, and it looks at how local *structures* and cultures, as well as local *agency*, shape the way cities negotiate changing forms of globalization.

- Taylor's *transformationalist* position provides a good counterpoint to the *globalist* accounts of globalization and cultural identity in Book 4, Chapter 2.

- Both readings bring the city as an agent into the politics of globalization – see Book 4, Chapter 4 on models of geo-governance.

Summary time! You should take the chance now to:

- Make sure you understand each of the points raised.

- Decide whether you disagree with any of them.

- Note any points of your own that we have missed or insufficiently developed, especially relevant links to Block 4.

SUMMARY

The city and globalization.

- The impact of globalization on cities is diverse, acting through economic, environmental, political, cultural and migratory structures. There are winners and losers between cities and within cities.

- Some global cities, such as London, have prospered economically at the price of intensified social polarization and disorder (see also Section 2.3).

- Some cities, especially older manufacturing centres, have been negatively affected, especially when disconnected from global financial and service networks.

- Cities, as agents and containers of local structures, have responded in different localized ways.

2.5 The city and knowledge

What kinds of connections and relationships between the city and knowledge can you think of?

Think about the way in which knowledge and communication was picked up in Sections 2.1 and 2.4 above.

Jot down any notes or ideas you have.

Our brainstorm came up with:

- Cities are key sites of knowledge production. Centres of scientific research, key religious institutions, universities, etc. are overwhelmingly – although not exclusively – located in cites.

- In fact, some cities in the UK are dominated by and defined by these relationships, e.g. Oxford, Cambridge, Canterbury.

- As we know from Section 2.1, the diversity, anonymity and heterogeneity of cities has significant impacts on the experience of urban living. Raban (Reading 1) highlights the importance of tacit cultural knowledge about signs, symbols and identities.

- In Section 2.4 we reviewed the idea of the city as a node in global, national and regional networks of economic and human flows – but also flows of communication.

We shall be returning to all of these relationships and ideas in more depth in Section 5 of this review. In this section, to consolidate and expand your understanding of the debate about the city in an era of advanced telecommunications and knowledge intense economies, we shall look at a reading by Peter Hall.

ACTIVITY 10

Read the article below by the geographer Peter Hall.

How does Hall think the advent of modern information technologies and new knowledge industries will affect cities?

- What are the enduring advantages of cities as sites of economic and cultural life?

- What connections can you make between his argument and the account of globalization developed in Block 4?

- Do you think Hall's argument applies to all cities in the UK? If not, why not?

Peter Hall: 'Cities of people and cities of bits'

Why do old cities like London and New York retain such a strong position in an age when information technology should have made cities obsolete?

The shift into a service producing economy has rendered old factors of production, such as coal deposits or long stretches of navigable water, ever less relevant to competitive advantage. Today's raw material is information: weightless, easily produced and equally easily exported. Once the individual, for example, has paid her user fee to log onto the World Wide Web, she thinks nothing of surfing three miles or three thousand miles along the Superhighway.

The effects of the information revolution are already being felt. In the UK, business activities are moving out of London to regional cities such as Leeds, Newcastle, and Glasgow. The growth of direct banking, especially in Leeds, has seen spectacular advances in the past five years. British Airways has recently moved its inquiry reservation service out of Heathrow and into Newcastle – where pecunious undergraduates with good southern accents service your every requirement. If you now phone for a domestic reservation, Britain's national carrier will connect you to a sales representative in Bombay. Best Western hotels use the inmates of the Arizona Women's penitentiary to take reservations. Once inside the informational world, the user rarely knows where she is – unless you happen to ask your service provider. [...]

So, what is left for this earthly world? What are the forces that will keep industries and services in major cities – centres which traditionally carry very high operating costs?

This is difficult territory. The experts in the field have by no means reached a conclusion. However enthusiastic they purport to be about the effects of new technology, they all seem to believe there is something in traditional cities after all, some special factor that allows them to win out against the all-conquering forces of cheap labour.

To understand why we have to recognise that the information revolution is not a zero-sum game where the computer beats the human interaction and where electronic communication can always act as an adequate substitute for face-to-face communication. Historical evidence indicates that the growth of telecommunications traffic is, in fact, paralleled by the growth of terrestrial human travel. Every programmed contact by telecommunications will lead to the need for an unprogrammed contact, i.e. face-to-face communication. The real question is whether this face-to-face contact takes place in a city, or at the Gatwick Hilton or the O'Hare Holiday Inn outside its boundaries.

The evidence seems to suggest that established capital cities enjoy the tremendous competitive advantage of inertia: because things have always been done in a particular location, they tend to remain there. The pattern is especially pronounced when activities depend on privileged information. A great deal of life in cities consists simply of the exchange of such information. Why is so much high value added economic activity concentrated in places like Silicon Valley? Why does the City of London exist when you can potentially trade from any location? The answer is that it is because of the exchange of special privileged information, be it in gyms, at dinner parties, or at the pub. There is strong anecdotal evidence that these qualities will go on operating and that businesses will happily continue to pay for it through high rents.

These factors are [...] general external economies, rather than external economies specific to the industry. They are of particular importance in complex, multi-industry cities like Paris, rather than single industry cities like Washington. [...] external economies arise precisely from that exchange of information across different business boundaries which London, Paris and Rome enjoy. These conversations could take place in other peripheral centres, but they don't because this activity has accumulated within established cities.

This doesn't mean geographical patterns are fixed for all time. London's positioning, for example, is not guaranteed. The decline of the global cities of Florence and Bruges from their *Quattrocento* dominance illustrates the dynamism of international civic power relations. But in the game of city competition there is a tangible inertia advantage, unless cities manage to completely destroy it through war or partition. The decline of Berlin after World War II is a spectacular case in point.

Competition between places, and particularly informational activities, will be the main driver of the economy in the foreseeable future, drawing places like New York, London and Los Angeles into increasing competition with each other – especially in the cultural and cultural technology industries, such as multi-media and interactive educational services. In the financial services sector, London will continue to compete with New York, Tokyo and perhaps in an EMU world Frankfurt.

Just as electronic informational activities can generate face-to-face activities, so they generate industries. Electronic exchange generates business tourism, which is itself an important component of the tourist industry. Electronic cultural information frequently generates the desire to see performances in reality [...] Where will all these related activities be located? The tremendous scale of inertia will ensure that traditional clusters of libraries, museums and tourist paraphernalia in major cities will indubitably benefit from this information revolution.

Globalisation will see the major cities retain their prominence – despite shedding some kinds of activity to lower order centres such as provincial capitals – by the compensatory growth of the highest order activities. Even the newest industries like multimedia are growing most strongly in small areas of Los Angeles and New York, although just as the film industry and popular music industry emerged in the relatively peripheral Hollywood and Memphis, new centres may become significant in combining culture and technology into new forms.

But the main conclusion is this. Where the newest industries are concerned the old categories are dwindling in their usefulness. The traditional 'mercantilist' argument over the competitiveness of the nation state is being increasingly superseded by debates about the competitiveness of city and regional economies. The international economic league table of the 1960s has been replaced by civic and regional prospectuses promising foreign investors best possible locations. It is to this kind of competition – a competition in which old cities retain great advantages even in the newest industries – that we should be turning our attention.

Source: Hall, 1996, pp.25–6

COMMENT

Our notes looked like this:

IMPACT OF GLOBAL INFORMATION TECHNOLOGY

1 Shift of business, esp. call centres, from London to regional cities – cheaper land and labour.

2 Shift of businesses to developing world/prisons!

BUT END OF THE CITY?

New telecoms leads to increasing human travel (cf. the telephone) but will the travel and meeting happen in old city centres or peripheries (i.e. Gatwick)?

ADVANTAGES OF THE CITY

1 Competitive advantage of inertia – things always done that way.

2 Importance of informal circulation of knowledge and information in cities – City of London, Silicon Valley.

3 Importance of conversations and exchange across many businesses and industries too.

4 Electronic industries will generate new industries/business which involve face-to-face meeting and travel – culture/education/tourism.

BLOCK 4

Hall is drawing on elements of the technological determinism of the account of the impact of the telegraph and Internet in Bk 4, Ch. 2, Sect. 5. Information technologies etc., rather than economic and political factors, are driving change.

Drawing on the globalist arguments across Block 4, Hall seems to be arguing that globalization will diminish the importance of nation-states and increase the importance of cities and regions as sites of economic activity and policy making. Cities will compete with each other rather than nations.

ALL OF THE UK?

Hard to say without more data, but the focus of the argument seems to be London and its relationship with the big provincial/regional cities of England.

The increasing importance of regions vis-à-vis nation-states could be said to be a factor behind the emergence of Cardiff and Edinburgh as capitals which bring not only status but also jobs, economic growth, etc.

Hold on to these arguments for a moment because we want to look briefly at another dimension of the relationship between cities and knowledge, one that connects to a host of arguments in Block 5 of the course: the role of expert knowledge in shaping cities. In the post-war UK, cities have been shaped unconsciously by broad social trends that have altered the physical fabric and economic and social life of the city: the advent of mass motoring, the move to the suburbs, and de-industrialization and the loss of manufacturing jobs in old cities. We will be looking at all of these issues in more detail in Section 3 of the review. Here we want to take a look at some of the conscious, deliberate forces and decisions involved in shaping cities; above all the role of urban planners, architects, local politicians, etc. In the post-war era the social standing and legitimacy of these groups has radically shifted and in the final decades of the twentieth century public trust in their urban plans, solutions and visions massively declined – a central theme of Block 5.

ACTIVITY 11

Go back to Reading 3, Allan Cochrane, 'Administered cities'. Skim the reading and your notes, and try and reframe the discussion in terms of the debate over expert knowledge, urban planning and urban design.

COMMENT

We noted this:

1 Urban planning/design can be thought of as a form of expert knowledge.

2 Post-war urban planning, drawing on the ideas of Le Corbusier, Ebenezer Howard, etc., claimed a privileged position in *knowing* what was good for cities and *knowing* how to achieve it.

3 The programme founded on their understanding of the inbuilt diversity of cities, their ignorance of major forces of structural change such as

globalization, motorization, de-industrialization, and their impact on other actors and agents in city politics and administration.

4 The experts have been challenged by new models of planning and administration with alternative, grass-roots democratic models – but often both have been outflanked by private economic agents.

Again, hold on to this, we will be returning to it in a moment. The time has now come to look back directly at your work on Block 5, before we synthesize it with our work on the city and knowledge.

ACTIVITY 12

Look back over your notes on Block 5. If you have not collected them together or reduced them, take the opportunity now to have a go. We are going to work with the same set of questions as we did in Section 2.1, Activity 2.

- What were the key questions of the block?
- In what ways were the course themes used?
- In what ways did each chapter in the block address these issues? What were the key debates in each chapter?
- What were the key case studies, the best examples, and the types of empirical evidence used?
- What additional materials from the audio-cassette and the TV programme can you use?

COMMENT

Our notes looked like this:

QUESTIONS

1 What is knowledge?
2 How is knowledge socially constructed?
3 Decline in trust of expert/elite knowledge?
4 Knowledge as a force of social change?

THEMES

U+D

Uncertainty and diversity very closely linked. Internal diversity of knowledge systems explored. Flowering of many competing knowledge systems in the same field explored. Both result in uncertainty amongst experts and this is communicated to the general public. Post-modernism, very strong argument about diversity and uncertainty; risk society similarly strong on uncertainty and conflict of interpretations centre stage.

S+A

Knowledge systems can act as structures, shaping agency - what we can and can't say/do/know. But also provide context for innovation, criticism, etc.

K+K

Narrative - explores origins and consequences of increasingly diverse knowledge systems. Impact of new knowledges and ways of seeing world on wider social structures.

Analytical - places circuit of knowledge and social science knowledge in a social context.

Contrast different systems of knowledge and knowing by method, evidence, etc., natural science, social science, common sense, religion, etc. Ch. 1 and Ch. 2.

Contrast different social science methods - positivism vs. interpretative social science in Ch. 2.

Returns to role of moral/normative political argument esp. Ch. 3.

Returns to problems of theory evaluation Ch. 4.

CHAPTERS AND DEBATES

Ch. 1

Explores knowledge of health and illness as example of general issues in social construction of knowledge.

Explores four models of sociology of knowledge: Popper, Kuhn, Foucault, and Fox Keller

Explores role of language, power, institutions and social change in constructing and validating knowledge.

Ch. 2

Explores social construction of religious knowledge, Weber vs. Durkheim, substantive vs. functional models of religion.

Contrasts positivist and interpretative social science as model of explanation and investigation.

Focuses on secularization debate, rise of new spirituality, role of ethnicity and gender.

Ch. 3

Explores diversity and uncertainly in realm of political ideologies.

Uses challenge of environmental problems and green arguments to highlight weakness and uncertainty amongst modern political ideological and political elites - example of declining trust?

Ch. 4

Explores knowledge as force for social change – contrasts knowledge society with fragmented society with risk society, explores different forms of uncertainty.

EVIDENCE AND EXAMPLES

Ch. 1

SIDS – contrasts soc. sci. and nat. sci.

Ch. 2

Quantitative data on church attendance and beliefs.

Qualitative data on new spirituality and meaning of religion.

Ch. 3

Key debates over economic, political, cultural challenges provide testing ground for strength and plausibility of political ideologies.

Ch. 4

NB workbook and cross-course refs provide the bulk of examples that relate to the three debates in the chapter.

AUDIO AND TV

TV 05 on parenting – sleep and MMR problems for parents. Note examples of diverse sources of expert information. Complexity of reading and using that information amongst public.

We will return to the analytical strand of knowledge and knowing in Section 5. Here we want to focus on the narrative strand.

To what extent does the fate of cities and urban planning parallel the wider social changes explored in Block 5?

We noted:

- The impact of information technology and globalization on the city described here could be interpreted through the lens of both the knowledge economy and post-Fordist debates in Book 5, Chapter 4, Sections 3 and 5. In this sense the city does not so much parallel other changes (such as changes in work, social life and order) but provides the main geographical location in which those changes work themselves out.

- The fate of urban planning as expert knowledge has clear parallels with the accounts of diversity/uncertainty, medicine/religion, and political ideologies.

- However, there are significant differences. Expert knowledge in the form of urban planning has been delegitimized by the perceived consequences of post-war urban development programmes, rather than internal diversity or epistemological exposure.

- Urban planners have never had the formal or informal power and authority of other professions, such as doctors, nor have they occupied institutional positions as powerful as those occupied by clerics or politicians.

- It may be urban planners' political weakness that makes their expert knowledge particularly vulnerable. Counter narratives of urban decline may overestimate their importance at the expense of wider patterns of urban social change.

Summary time! You should take the chance now to:

- Make sure you understand each of the points raised.

- Decide whether you disagree with any of them.

- Note any points of your own that we have missed or insufficiently developed, especially relevant links to Block 5.

SUMMARY

The city and knowledge.

- Cities, in diverse ways, have been transformed by information technology, and new knowledge networks and industries, combining with processes of globalization, de-industrialization and social polarization.

- Cities have been shaped by a struggle between different ways of knowing and imagining cities.

- Expert urban design and planning knowledge has suffered a major decline in public authority and political power, though it was always limited and constrained.

- The contemporary diversity of urban actors and models of governance have yet to produce a consensus on cities or find ways of effectively regulating inequalities in power and cities.

Take a breath, literally or metaphorically or both. Audio-cassette 10, Side A is a moment to pause and reflect. The conversation between Kath Woodward, David Goldblatt and Hugh Mackay gives you the opportunity to think through your strategy for completing the *End of Course Review* and TMA 06.

 Please listen to Audio-cassette 10, Side A and return to this point in the *End of Course Review*.

The key points for you to consider are:

- Now is a good time to look at the student notes for TMA 06.

- You need to start thinking about which one of the three options on TMA 06 you are going to do.

- You need to think about how much time you've got to do Sections 3–5 and cut your cloth accordingly.

3 UNCERTAINTY AND DIVERSITY IN THE POST-WAR UK CITY

3.1 Revisiting uncertainty and diversity

One of the main functions of the course theme of *uncertainty and diversity* has been to allow you to explore the extent of economic, social, political, and cultural change in the UK in the latter half of the twentieth century and to encourage you, as a social scientist, to think historically. Above all, it has provided a means of raising important questions about this period. We began the process of reviewing uncertainty and diversity in the *Mid Course Review* where we drew up a summary of its use in the first four blocks of the course; this is reproduced as Table 1.

TABLE 1   Uncertainty and diversity: Introductory Block–Block 3

Course material	Uncertainty	Diversity
Introductory Chapter	Fear of crime and sense of insecurity on the rise?	Moral panics as response to threats of deviant diversity.
Book 1, Chapter 1	Old gender, class identities under challenge as social structures change. Re-evaluation of age/body as source of identity – norms of youth able-bodiedness challenged.	Collective action leads to creation and entrenchment of new cultural identities.
Book 1, Chapter 2	New patterns of gender identity, uncertainty for boys?	Fuzzy categories, new opportunities for girls?
Book 1, Chapter 3	Increasing complexity of economic structures makes old class identities less plausible.	Consumption-based identities suggest greater diversity of identities possible.
Book 1, Chapter 4	Devolution, end of Empire, etc. Britishness and Englishness more uncertain identities.	Promise of multiculturalism but persistent blockage of racism, individual and institutional.
TV 01: *Defining Moments*	What does it mean to be British in the 1990s? What rituals are appropriate for national occasions?	Diana's funeral appears to encompass and represent a much more diverse nation than the establishment at Churchill's funeral.
Book 2, Chapter 2	Dominance of medical model and expert medical knowledge challenged and undermined.	Medical model challenged by diverse health belief systems.

Course material	Uncertainty	Diversity
Book 2, Chapter 4	Environmental dangers with unpredictable consequences appear to be on the rise. Expert scientific and political knowledge challenged.	
TV 02: *The Unusual Suspects*		Changing attitudes and definitions of disability lead to huge diversity of lives for people with disabilities.
Book 3, Chapter 2	Position of men in families and male identities more uncertain.	Family forms increasingly complex and diverse.
Book 3, Chapter 3	Increasingly flexible work makes working lives more uncertain.	Workforce increasingly gender diverse. Forms of work more complex.
Book 3, Chapter 4	Security delivered by post-war welfare state brought into question.	Welfare state forced to confront and respond to more diverse families, lifestyles, working lives.
TV 03: *Living with Risk*	Evidence of insecurity and complexity in the labour market.	

How can we begin to synthesize all of this material? It seems to us that, in general, many of these debates about uncertainty and diversity are linked to a common narrative. At the core of this interlocking narrative is the contrast between the contemporary experience of uncertainty and diversity and an earlier era of certainty and uniformity; what is often depicted as a 'golden age'. In both eras the two terms reinforce each other. A uniform society was simpler, offering less choices and therefore it underwrote certainties about who we were, what we could do and expect, etc. Similarly, with the emergence of a more diverse society the answers to the same questions became more complex and more uncertain.

As the summary in Table 1 shows, it wasn't merely uniformity that delivered certainty in these narratives. The post-war years have often been depicted as an era of social stability of secure, functioning institutions and established reliable patterns of behaviour. Low crime, full employment, a benign welfare state, and trusted systems of expert knowledge: scientists, doctors, politicians, etc. These have been counterpoised to an era of unstable, dysfunctional institutions, unreliable and anti-social behaviour, a collapse in trust in expert knowledge systems and their simple dichotomies. What has linked these two eras has been fundamental patterns of *social change*. A simplified story might suggest that there has been a direct shift from the 'certainty' of the 'golden age' to contemporary uncertainties.

However, we have consistently argued that all of these elements need to be challenged and unpacked. In particular, the sceptical social scientist might ask:

- Was there a 'golden age'? What is the evidence? What forms of uncertainty and conflict existed in the immediate post-war era?

- Where there has been change, has the emergence of social diversity been the driving force, or are other factors significant?

- Is the new era quite so bad? Diversity, in particular, can be a force for liberation, choice, etc. Are we actually more insecure, or do we merely feel more insecure?

- Above all, how does this narrative depend on who you are asking and what you are studying?

Before we think about these questions in relation to the city it would be useful to expand our coverage of uncertainty and diversity to include the work you have done on Blocks 4 and 5.

Take a look at the notes summarizing Blocks 4 and 5 that you made in Sections 2.4 and 2.5. Where in the blocks was *uncertainty and diversity* dealt with?

Have a look at your notes and compare them with our table below.

TABLE 2   Uncertainty and diversity: Blocks 4 and 5

Course material	Uncertainty	Diversity
Book 4, Chapter 2	Are the consequences of cultural globalization as straightforward as common sense might suggest?	Does cultural globalization create a more unified, homogenous global culture, or create a diversity of new hybrid cultures?
Book 4, Chapter 3	Does economic globalization produce greater uncertainty and instability in the world economic system? Does it make the power and autonomy of nation-states more uncertain?	
Book 4, Chapter 4	Has the decline of the old Westphalian order produced a more unruly, unregulatable global political system? Are new forms of geo-governance a potential source of stability and certainty?	Increasing range and diversity of international actors. Not just nation-states, but individuals, international institutions, etc.
TV 04		Games culture and the Japanese experience of both unifying and hybridizing cultural forms. The diversity of global flows.
Book 5, Chapter 1	Legitimacy and authority of medicine and science, challenged and undermined.	Complementary medicine new sources of knowledge.
Book 5, Chapter 2	Decline of trust in religious knowledge and dominant moral codes.	Emergence of a greater range of spiritual frameworks and belief systems in post-war UK.
Book 5, Chapter 3	Decline of trust in political elites, uncertainty regarding dominant political ideologies and their capacity to cope with new issues such as the environment.	New sources of knowledge and political action about the environment.
Book 5, Chapter 4	Post-modernists and post-Fordists point to a collapse of certainty in all epistemological frameworks and discourses. Advocates of a risk society argue that safety experts and environmental knowledge produce uncertainty rather than certainty in current era.	
TV 05	Uncertainty regarding the knowledge of health care professionals of all kinds and government agencies as well, especially MMR case study.	Range of parenting advice and belief systems indicates greater diversity in parenting knowledge and advice.

Where else in Section 2 of the *End of Course Review* have we touched on issues of *uncertainty and diversity* in general?

A quick scan suggested a few important connections:

- Section 2.1 – the city as a source of uncertain identities.

- Section 2.3 – grand plans as an attempt to impose certainty and uniformity from above; and in the USA other models of planning that encourage and celebrate diversity.

Hold on to these ideas and any other connections you have noted as you work through the rest of this section.

So, how do these debates illuminate the experience of the city in the post-war UK, and how in turn can an account of the city enrich our general understanding of the issues raised? Let's begin by asking if the study of change in the cities of the post-war UK lends support to the idea of a 'golden age'; an age of certainty which, under pressure from patterns of social change, has turned to an era of urban uncertainty and disorder.

The United Kingdom is not a rural society. By any definition or measure the vast majority of UK citizens live in cities or urban settings. Further, the UK has been an urbanized society for longer than any other country. Yet, in a great number of the UK's large cities, there are many people who wish to escape from what is widely perceived to be the 'disorder' of urban life, and in the process they are contributing to counter-urbanization and to the declining population of several UK cities. Stories of crime in the city abound (Fyfe, 1997). There is evidence that people are becoming increasingly hostile to the polluted environment that is a feature of many urban locations. Some are no longer prepared to put up with the daily grind of hours spent in congested traffic, with long delays on the dilapidated public transport system, and with general feelings of isolation, vulnerability and uncertainty about life in the city. Some areas of UK cities contain the highest levels of unemployment, the most intense poverty, and some of the worst housing conditions. If one needs to find any more evidence that cities are often viewed negatively then we need to look no further than the plethora of reports, studies, investigations and government policies which are targeted on particular aspects of urban life: 'Cities in Crisis' has been a regular banner headline in recent times. But, there is plenty of room for scepticism.

- When exactly was there a 'golden age' of cities in the UK?

- Are we all queuing up to leave the city?

- Is it possible for every group to leave the city, or is this the preserve of those who have the material means to do so?

- Are 'our' cities so bad in any case; are they not also places of excitement and vitality? Is 'rural life' always such a positive experience?

- Are these 'problems of the cities' problems for everyone?

These debates are not new. In fact, the depiction of the city as a source of disorder, a place of danger and social dislocation runs deep in English culture in particular. As we know from our study of Englishness (Book 1, Chapter 4, Section 6), the nation has predominantly been cast in rural terms, although it has long ceased to be a predominantly rural society. It is not surprising then, that a society with a deep-rooted anti-urbanism should often cast its attitude to cities in terms of 'golden ages' giving way to decline, disorder and fragmentation.

The rest of Section 3 sketches an outline history of urban change in the post-war UK that takes our crude 'golden age' narrative as its starting point, but subjects it to sceptical interrogation. In addition, each sub-section will ask you to draw on other work on *uncertainty and diversity* in DD100, including Section 2 of this review. The structure of the argument is set out in Figure 3.

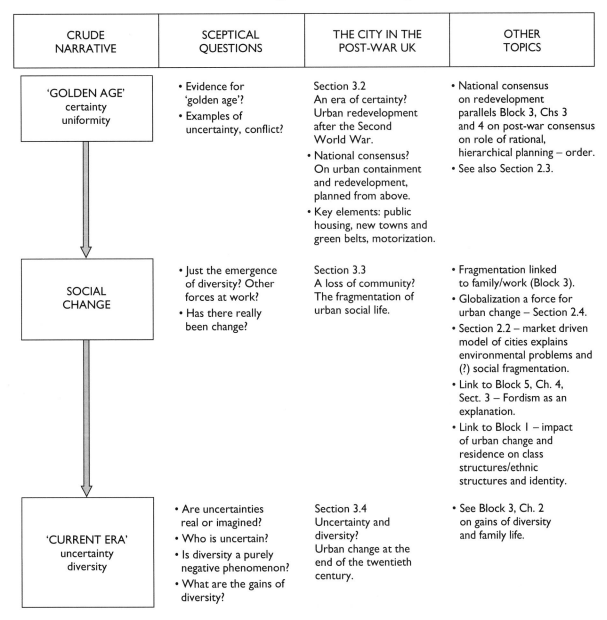

CRUDE NARRATIVE	SCEPTICAL QUESTIONS	THE CITY IN THE POST-WAR UK	OTHER TOPICS
'GOLDEN AGE' certainty uniformity	• Evidence for 'golden age'? • Examples of uncertainty, conflict?	Section 3.2 An era of certainty? Urban redevelopment after the Second World War. • National consensus? On urban containment and redevelopment, planned from above. • Key elements: public housing, new towns and green belts, motorization.	• National consensus on redevelopment parallels Block 3, Chs 3 and 4 on post-war consensus on role of rational, hierarchical planning – order. • See also Section 2.3.
SOCIAL CHANGE	• Just the emergence of diversity? Other forces at work? • Has there really been change?	Section 3.3 A loss of community? The fragmentation of urban social life.	• Fragmentation linked to family/work (Block 3). • Globalization a force for urban change – Section 2.4. • Section 2.2 – market driven model of cities explains environmental problems and (?) social fragmentation. • Link to Block 5, Ch. 4, Sect. 3 – Fordism as an explanation. • Link to Block 1 – impact of urban change and residence on class structures/ethnic structures and identity.
'CURRENT ERA' uncertainty diversity	• Are uncertainties real or imagined? • Who is uncertain? • Is diversity a purely negative phenomenon? • What are the gains of diversity?	Section 3.4 Uncertainty and diversity? Urban change at the end of the twentieth century.	• See Block 3, Ch. 2 on gains of diversity and family life.

FIGURE 3   Section 3: structure of the argument

3.2   An era of certainty? Urban redevelopment after the Second World War

In material terms it would be very hard to describe the 1940s and 1950s as a 'golden age'. Britain's cities had been scarred, albeit unevenly, by the calamitous economic decline of the 1930s. Although the war had brought new employment it had also left huge infrastructural scars on the urban landscape. In the north of England, central Scotland and south Wales, in what was then increasingly referred to as 'outer Britain', cities' economies were dominated by industries in relative decline. Further, overcrowding and decaying slums were seen by policy makers and organizations such as the Town Planning Movement and the Garden City Movement as particular problems which needed to be addressed. In Glasgow in 1945, for example, 700,000 people were living at an average density of 400 per acre, a figure which reached up to 700 in certain places. 'Something had to be done' about the UK's cities.

ACTIVITY 13

Read through the following speech made by Lewis Silkin, Minster of Town and Country Planning, in Parliament in 1947. It provides many pointers to the dominant thinking which characterized 'official' attitudes towards cities at the time.

How was 'the urban problem' presented and what 'solutions' were put forward to address this?

> The main objectives of town and country planning [...] are to secure a proper balance between competing demands for land, so that all the land of the country is used in the best interests of the whole people [...] Land will be needed for the housing programme, including the clearance of slums and the rebuilding of blitzed areas, the redevelopment of obsolete and badly laid out areas, the dispersal of population and industry from our large, overcrowded cities to new towns [...]

> On the other hand, town and country planning must preserve land from development. A high level of agricultural production is vital. More land must be kept for forestry [...] And it is important to safeguard the beauty of the countryside and coastline in order to enable more people to enjoy them [...]

> [...] the conflicting demands for land must be dovetailed together. If each is considered in isolation, the common interest is bound to suffer. Housing must be so located in relation to industry that workers are not compelled to make long, tiring and expensive journeys to and from work. Nor must our already large towns be permitted to sprawl, and expand, so as to eat up the adjacent rural areas and make access to the countryside and to the amenities in the centre of town more difficult. Green belts must be left around towns, and the most fertile land kept for food production. The continued drift from the countryside must be arrested [...] Between the wars, industry tended to concentrate in the South of

England, with the result that towns in the South, especially London, grew too large for health, efficiency and safety, while some of the older industrial areas suffered chronic unemployment.

(Official Report, 1946–47, Vol. 432; Second Reading of the Town and Country Planning Bill, 29 January 1947, Cmnd. 947 et seq.)

COMMENT

What did you note about the language used in the speech; in particular the use of terms such as 'whole people' or the 'common interest'?

The 1947 Town and Country Planning Act was couched in the language of what has been termed the post-war 'consensus' (see the discussion in Book 3, pp.118–28). 'National' or 'public' interests were part of the dominant social democratic ideology of the time. 'Everyone' would benefit from the better planning of 'our cities', and the process of planning was to be part and parcel of a wider programme of social reconstruction. However, despite the language employed by government ministers and the various semi-official bodies referred to above, competing regional and class interests shaped the redevelopment of urban Britain at this time, especially with regard to the ownership and control of land. Land ownership was an issue that was left largely untouched by government policy.

In Silkin's speech we can detect three main elements of immediate post-war urban policy:

- First, 'urban containment' to prevent further 'uncontrolled urbanization'. This was identified as a major problem in the 1930s and 1940s and was typified by rapid suburbanization and city 'sprawl'. In turn this was viewed as 'destroying the countryside'. The primary means of preventing this was the creation of 'green belts' around many of the UK's major cities.

- Second, 'regional balance'. This policy represented an attempt to address the contrasting fortunes of different parts of the UK, in particular the growing disparities in economic performance which had been a feature of the 1930s.

- The third element which we can identify is urban reconstruction or, to use the language of the time, 'redevelopment'.

Policies of regional balance are beyond our scope – although we do refer to the impact of regional policies on cities in Section 4 in relation to the redevelopment of Cardiff. Here we want to concentrate on the policies of urban containment and urban redevelopment which were to have a profound and lasting impact on the landscape of urban Britain.

In response to the perceived and interlinked problems of urban sprawl destroying the countryside and urban overcrowding as generating social problems, urban policy attempted to relieve both. Sprawl would be countered by the creation of 'green belts' around urban areas where building would be highly restricted. New developments, to take the 'overspill' populations of the old cities, would be focused in satellite new towns, whose blank slate would provide the opportunity for rational and benign planning and design models (see Figure 4 for the example of London). Within cities, old overcrowded inner-city slums would be demolished and the population rehoused in lower density, often high-rise inner estates and increasingly in new built peripheral estates. The first strategy was led by newly created government quangos – the new town commissions – whilst the second strategy was led by local authorities and their housing departments. The extent of the public building programme can be seen in Table 3; as can its eventual demise.

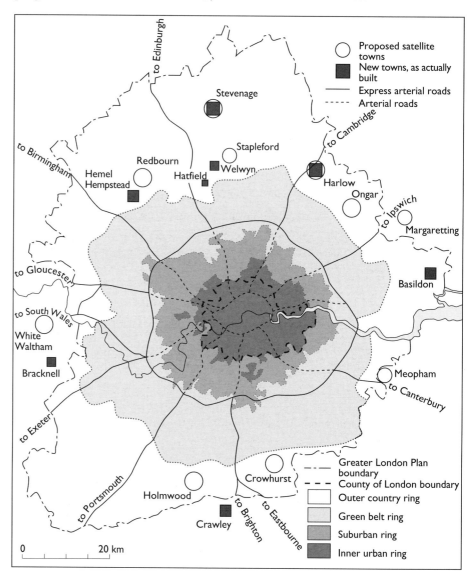

FIGURE 4   The Abercrombie Plan for Greater London, 1944

Source: Massey *et al.*, 1999, p.14

TABLE 3 Categories of housing tenure and stock of dwellings (in millions) in Great Britain, 1914–91

Date	Rented from local authority or new town		Privately rented		Owner-occupied		Total number of dwellings
	No.	%	No.	%	No.	%	
1914	0.1	1.8	7.5	88.2	0.9	10.0	8.5
1944	1.6	12.4	8.0	62.0	3.3	25.6	12.9
1951	2.5	17.9	7.3	52.5	4.1	29.6	13.9
1961	4.4	26.8	5.0	30.5	7.0	42.7	16.4
1971	5.8	30.6	3.6	18.9	9.6	50.5	19.0
1981	6.6	31.0	2.7	12.6	11.9	56.4	21.2
1991	5.7	24.8	1.7	7.4	15.6	67.7	23.1

Source: Carter, 1995

The extent of this redevelopment can also be judged from figures provided by Andrew Cox (1984). Cox estimated that by 1962 one-third of urban areas with a population of more than 500,000 were involved in some kind of development scheme, one-half of areas with a population of between 40,000 and 100,000, and one-quarter of areas with a population of between 20,000 and 40,000 were similarly involved. However, quantity of redevelopment did not necessarily translate into quality. New towns were to represent, in the words of the Reith Report (1946), 'balanced communities for working and living'. 'Balance' was primarily viewed in class terms, the mixing of people from different social backgrounds, here meaning occupations. However, UK new towns were to be characterized both by their selectivity of residents and, of course, not everyone was in a position to move from the cities. In the early years in the 1950s and 1960s, their populations were skewed towards younger, more skilled social groups, and were noticeable for the very low proportions of residents from minority ethnic groups. Overspill estates, on the other hand, tended to accommodate more semi and unskilled workers. The result of all this was, according to Hall *et al.* (1973, p.397), 'the development of publicly sanctioned, publicly subsidized apartheid'.

We will explore the impact of the shifts in Section 3.3, but it is worth noting that perhaps the most significant force on the shape of the post-war city was being unintentionally unleashed, almost unnoticed in this era: the massive increase in car ownership in the 1940s and 1950s. Between 1940 and 1960 the number of cars on UK roads increased from 2,300,000 to 9,400,000. Ring roads, motorways and other large road schemes were soon to become a pervasive feature of urban Britain.

Take a moment to review this short account of urban policy in the post-war UK.

- How does it compare with our crude narrative?
- What connections did you note to earlier course materials on *uncertainty and diversity*?

Jot down your notes and then take a look at our Diagram F.

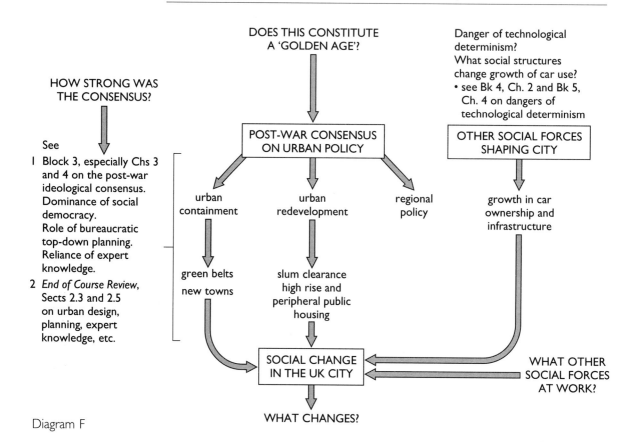

Diagram F

3.3 A loss of 'community'? The fragmentation of urban social life

Let's take a closer look at some of the sceptical questions raised in Diagram I. First, what changes were there in UK cities in the first couple of decades after the war? For the big cities of the UK the demographic changes appear clear. Population 'overspill' and out-migration from the cities meant that during the 1960s alone the population of the main conurbations – London, West Midlands, Merseyside, Greater Manchester, Tyneside, West Yorkshire and Clydeside – declined by 9 per cent on average. Brian Robson (1988) estimates that between 1951 and 1981 the large cities lost on average one-third of their population. The new towns and urban redevelopment policies involved a significant restructuring of urban life, and in particular the destruction of older working-class areas of cities. It was in this context that concerns about 'a loss of community' can be a way of referring to the perceived effects of social and economic change, and the period in question was, as we have seen, a period of major change.

Urban change in the post-war UK provided a rich opportunity for social scientists to study the effects of social change. One notable school of the social sciences in this era became known as 'community studies'. This referred to a variety of research of mainly working-class 'communities' undergoing industrial and/or physical change. One of the best known community studies was *Family and Kinship in East London* by Michael Young and Peter Willmott. This explored the impact of social change on familial life among families moving from Bethnal Green, in East London, to the new Greenleigh housing estate outside London in the 1950s.

ACTIVITY 14

Read the extracts below from Michael Young and Peter Willmott's study.

In what ways was the sense of a loss of community explained and articulated at the time?

Michael Young and Peter Willmott: 'Family and kinship in East London'

Keeping themselves to themselves

We have now described some of the effects of migration. People's relatives are no longer neighbours sharing the intimacies of daily life. Their new neighbours are strangers, drawn from every part of the East End, and they are, as we have seen, treated with reserve. In point of services, neighbours do not make up for kin.

Our informants were so eager to talk about their neighbours and generally about their attitude to other residents on the estate, that we feel bound to report them. They frequently complained of the unfriendliness of the place, which they found all the more mysterious because it was so different from Bethnal Green. Why should Greenleigh be considered unfriendly? This chapter tries to explain.

The prevailing attitude is expressed by Mr Morrow. 'You can't get away from it, they're not so friendly down here. It's not "Hello, Joe," "Hello, mate." They pass you with a side-glance as though they don't know you.' And by Mr Adams. 'We all come from the slums, not Park Lane, but they don't mix. In Bethnal Green you always used to have a little laugh on the doorstep. There's none of that in Greenleigh. You're English, but you feel like a foreigner here, I don't know why. Up there you'd lived for years, and you knew how to deal with the people there. People here are different.' And by Mr Prince. 'The neighbours round here are very quiet. They all keep themselves to themselves. They all come from the East End but they all seem to change when they come down here.'

Of the forty-one couples, twenty-three considered that other people were unfriendly, eight were undecided one way or another, and ten considered them friendly: the recorded opinions are those of the couples, because in no interview did husband and wife appear to hold strongly different views. How does this majority who consider their fellow residents unfriendly feel about themselves? Do they also label themselves unfriendly? No one admits it, some indignantly deny it. If they are hostile themselves, they do not acknowledge it, but attribute the feeling to others. Yet they mostly reveal that their own behaviour is the same as they resent in others; that (since *others* are unfriendly) to withdraw will avoid trouble and keep the peace; that co-existence is safer, because more realistic, than cooperation. 'The policy here is don't have a lot to do with each other, then there won't be any trouble,' says Mr Chortle succinctly. [...]

No doubt if they all came from Bethnal Green, they would get on much better than they do: many of them would have known each other before and, anyway, at least have a background in common. As it is, they arrive from all over London, though with East Enders predominant. Such a vast common origin might be enough to bind together a group of Cockneys in the Western Desert; Western Essex is too near for that. When all are from London, no one is from London: they are from one of the many districts into which the city is divided. What is then emphasized is far more their difference than their sameness. The native of Bethnal Green feels himself different from the native of Stepney or Hackney. One of our informants, who had recently moved into Bethnal Green from Hackney, a few minutes away, told us 'I honestly don't like telling people I live in Bethnal Green. I come from Hackney myself, and when I was a child living in Hackney, my parents wouldn't let me come to Bethnal Green. I thought it was something terrible.' These distinctions are carried over to Greenleigh, where it is no virtue in a neighbour to have come from Stepney, rather the opposite. Mr Abbot summed it up as follows: 'You've not grown up with them. They come from different neighbourhoods, they're different sorts of people, and they don't mix.'

We had expected that, despite these disadvantages, people would, in the course of time, settle down and make new friendships, and our surprise was that this had not happened to a greater extent. The informants who had been on the estate longest had no higher opinion than others of the friendliness of their fellows. Four of the eighteen couples who had been there six or seven years judged other people to be friendly, as did six of the twenty-three couples with residence for five years or less. Mr Wild was one who commented on how long it was taking for time its wonders to perform.

> 'They're all Londoners here but they get highbrow when they get here. They're not so friendly. Coming from a turning like the one where we lived, we knew everyone. We were bred and born amongst them, like one big family we were. We knew all their troubles and everything. Here they are all total strangers to each other and so they are all wary of each other. It's a question of time, I suppose. But we've been here four years and I don't see any change yet. It does seem to be taking a very long while to get friendly.'

One reason it is taking so long is that the estate is so strung out – the number of people per acre at Greenleigh being only one-fifth what it is in Bethnal Green – and low density does not encourage sociability.

In Bethnal Green your pub, and your shop, is a 'local'. There people meet their neighbours. At Greenleigh they are put off by the distance. They don't go to the pub because it may take twenty minutes to walk, instead of one minute as in Bethnal Green. They don't go to the shops, which are grouped into specialized centres instead of being scattered in converted houses through the ordinary streets,[1] more than they have to, again because of the distance. And they don't go so much to either because when they get there, the people are gathered from the corners of the estate, instead of being neighbours with whom they already have a point of contact. The pubs and shops of Bethnal Green serve so well as 'neighbourhood centres' because there are so many of them: they provide the same small face-to-face groups with continual opportunities to meet. Where they are few and large, as at Greenleigh, they do not serve this purpose so well.

From people to house

The relatives of Bethnal Green have not, therefore, been replaced by the neighbours of Greenleigh. The newcomers are surrounded by strangers instead of kin. Their lives outside the family are no longer centred on people; their lives are centred on the house. This change from a people-centred to a house-centred existence is one of the fundamental changes resulting from the migration. It goes some way to explain the competition for status which is in itself the result of isolation from kin and the cause of estrangement from neighbours, the reason why co-existence, instead of being just a state of neutrality – a tacit agreement to live and let live – is frequently infused with so much bitterness.

When we asked what in their view had made people change since they moved from East London, time and time again our informants gave the same kind of suggestive answers that people had become, as they put it, 'toffee-nosed', 'big headed', 'high and mighty', 'jealous', 'a cut above everybody else'. [...]

The reason they do not want to leave the borough is that its effectiveness depends a good deal upon the geographical proximity of the key figures. During the stages of their lives when they are most in need of support, neither wives nor their mothers can easily move about. If they have babies and young children to look after, the wives cannot readily make longer journeys than they can easily navigate with a pram. Nor can aged parents easily travel far. The mobility of both is often small. This is all the more severe a limitation if they have little money to pay for transport, and little of the time-sense and organizing power which enable some people to maintain a kind of cohesion in a widely scattered circle of friends and relatives. Migration by young couples interposes a barrier of distance which impedes the reciprocal flow of services between the generations. Hence the significance of the move of only a few miles to Greenleigh. [...]

The physical size of reconstruction is so great that the authorities have been understandably intent upon bricks and mortar. Their negative task is to demolish slums which fall below the most elementary standards of hygiene, their positive one to build new houses and new towns cleaner and more spacious than the old. Yet even when the town planners have set themselves to create communities anew as well as houses, they have still put their faith in buildings, sometimes speaking as though all that was necessary for neighbourliness was a neighbourhood unit, for community spirit a community centre. If this were so, then there would be no harm in shifting people about the country, for what is lost could soon be regained by skilful architecture and design. But there is surely more to a community than that. The sense of loyalty to each other amongst the inhabitants of a place like Bethnal Green is not due to buildings. It is due far more to ties of kinship and friendship which connect the *people* of one household to the *people* of another. In such a district community spirit does not have to be fostered, it is already there. If the authorities regard that spirit as a social asset worth preserving, they will not uproot more people, but build the new houses around the social groups to which they already belong.

Footnote

1. Out of the 1,214 shops in Bethnal Green in 1955, 766 had living accommodation attached to them, and only 458 were of the lock-up type of Greenleigh.

Source: Young and Willmott, 1986 edn, pp.147–99

COMMENT

The Bethnal Green study suggested that some people who moved from older working-class areas of cities to new towns and overspill housing estates often found it difficult to adapt to the 'new life'. Many of the new housing developments initially represented little more than mass housing dormitories, with few social amenities. Employment was often to be found some distance away, and could only be accessed at considerable costs in terms of travel. Feelings of isolation and being 'cut-off' were frequently recorded sentiments in a number of the studies of life in new housing developments during this time. Young and Willmott argued that while the transition to new estates may disrupt family and kinship ties, new networks could also be established in these locations. But the idea that there was a 'lack of community' on new estates and in new towns was a widespread sentiment at the time.

So, some sociological research suggests that the post-war vision of balanced communities and social improvement had resulted in social fragmentation – a line of argument that has, in part, recast the past in terms of past 'golden ages' and contemporary fragmentation and uncertainty – a narrative described by David Lee and Howard Newby as follows:

Since the 1960s a widespread sense of 'loss of community' has arisen in many urban areas, caused either by changes in the social composition of their population or by their physical redevelopment. In many cities old-established, mostly working-class neighbourhoods have been bulldozed aside and their former inhabitants decanted into new housing estates and high-rise flats which have drawn frequent accusations of being 'soul-less' and lacking any of the 'community spirit' which is alleged to have existed among Victorian back-to-back terraces. The stereotype of the dreary, windswept, monotonous, modern housing development has entered public demonology as the very antithesis of what is commonly understood by 'community'. Ironically many of the old urban neighbourhoods which are now revered as intimate and vital communities were the same areas that were greeted with such suspicion by so many nineteenth-century commentators!

(Lee and Newby, 1983, p.55)

This short account of community studies research only addresses some of our sceptical questions – it certainly leaves open the question of what social forces, alongside urban redevelopment programmes, have been at work in shaping the post-war UK.

On Audio-cassette 10, Side B is a conversation between David Goldblatt, Doreen Massey (Professor of Geography at the OU) and Ken Worpole (writer and researcher on urban issues). The conversation is structured around seven key questions which all speak to the issues we've been addressing in this section.

ACTIVITY 15

As you listen, note down your responses to the following:

1 What are the roots of anti-urbanism in English/British culture?

2 Has there ever been a 'golden age' of cities in the UK?

3 Was the impact of the post-war programme of urban redevelopment purely negative?

4 What other forces and processes reshaped the UK's cities from the 1960s onwards?

5 How great a diversity in social change has there been between the UK's cities?

6 What were the key features of urban change and governance in the 1980s and 1990s?

7 What alternative models of urban development are being proposed?

 Now listen to Audio-cassette 10, Side B and return to this point in the *End of Course Review.*

C O M M E N T _____

We noted:

1   Anti-urbanism.

Rural aristocratic dominance in UK/English culture. NB existence of pro-urbanism in UK culture.

2 'Golden age'?
  Possibly Victorian cities – but civic regeneration and enormous
  poverty sat side by side.

3 Impact redevelopment.
  Not entirely negative, much creditable public sector housing.

4 Other forces:
  (a) De-industrialization, rise of service sector.
  (b) Migration, esp. New Commonwealth.
  (c) Motorization, but significant support and subsidy economically,
      politically.

5 Diversity between cities.
  Contrast: industrial vs. post-industrial cities (esp. hi-tech cities).
  Seaside towns.

We will come to our responses to questions 6 and 7 in the next sub-section.

ACTIVITY 16

Before you move on, take a moment to look at the data in Tables 4 and 5 below
– how could you use these data to support, qualify or contradict the claims made
about urban change in the UK on Audio-cassette 10, Side B?

TABLE 4　Population change for eight large cities, 1901–88

City	1988 population (000s)	Change rate for period				
		1901–51 %	51–61 %	61–71 %	71–81 %	81–88 %
Birmingham	993.7	+49.1	+1.9	−7.2	−8.3	−2.4
Glasgow	703.2	+24.9	−2.9	−13.8	−22.0	−9.2
Leeds	709.6	+19.3	+2.5	+3.6	−4.6	−1.2
Liverpool	469.6	+10.9	−5.5	−18.2	−16.4	−9.2
London	6,735.4	+25.9	−2.5	−6.8	−9.9	−1.0
Manchester	445.9	+8.3	−5.9	−17.9	−17.5	−3.6
Newcastle upon Tyne	279.6	+26.1	−2.3	−8.4	−9.9	−1.6
Sheffield	528.3	+23.0	+0.4	−2.1	−6.1	−3.6
Eight cities total	10,865.3	+25.0	−2.1	−7.9	−10.9	−2.4
Great Britain	55,486.4	+32.1	+5.0	+5.3	+0.6	+1.3

Source: Champion and Townsend, 1990, p.161

TABLE 5   Changes in employment by sector and type of area in Great Britain, 1951–81

Sector and periods	Inner cities		Outer cities		Free-standing cities		Small towns and rural areas		Great Britain	
	(000s)	(%)	(000s)	(%)	(000s)	(%)	(000s)	(%)	(000s)	(%)
Manufacturing										
1951–61	−143	−8.0	+84	+5.0	−21	−2.0	+453	+14.0	+374	+5.0
1961–71	−428	−26.1	−217	−10.3	−93	−6.2	+498	+12.5	−255	−3.9
1971–81	−447	−36.8	−480	−32.6	−311	−28.6	−717	−17.2	−1,929	−24.5
Private services										
1951–61	+192	+11.0	+110	+11.0	+128	+17.0	+514	+16.0	+944	+14.0
1961–71	−297	−15.3	+92	+8.1	−7	−0.8	+535	+14.5	+318	+4.2
1971–81	−105	−6.4	+170	+17.3	+91	+10.9	+805	+24.8	+958	+14.4
Public services										
1951–61	+13	+1.0	+54	+7.0	+38	+6.0	+200	+8.0	+302	+6.0
1961–71	+25	+2.0	+170	+21.6	+110	+17.7	+502	+17.3	+807	+14.5
1971–81	−78	−7.4	+102	+8.8	+53	+6.5	+456	+14.1	+488	+7.7
Total employment										
1951–61	+43	+1.0	+231	+6.0	+140	+6.0	+1,060	+10.0	+1,490	+7.0
1961–71	−643	−14.8	+19	+0.6	+54	+2.4	+1,022	+8.5	+320	+1.3
1971–81	−538	−14.6	−236	−7.1	−150	−5.4	+404	+3.5	−590	−2.7

Source: Hausner, 1987, p.7

3.4 Uncertainty and diversity? Urban change in the 1980s and 1990s

Look back to Diagram F on p.78 of this review. How could we add the arguments of Section 3.3 and Audio-cassette 10, Side B to it, especially the breakdown of the post-war consensus, its replacement by an alternative framework, and its current limits?

Returning to questions 6 and 7 from Audio-cassette 10, Side B (Activity 15), our response is shown in Diagram G.

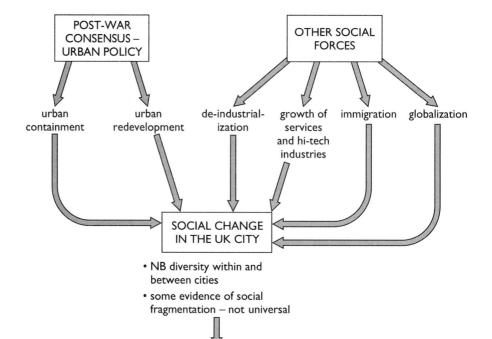

POST-WAR CONSENSUS – URBAN POLICY

OTHER SOCIAL FORCES

urban containment

urban redevelopment

de-industrialization

growth of services and hi-tech industries

immigration

globalization

SOCIAL CHANGE IN THE UK CITY

- NB diversity within and between cities
- some evidence of social fragmentation – not universal

1980s BREAK WITH POST-WAR CONSENSUS

- rejection of state planning/provision
- inner-city taskforces, especially after 1980s riots
- quangos and private sector take lead

SOCIAL CHANGE IN THE UK CITY

- traffic problem reaches crisis point
- urban sprawl intensifies
- destruction of public space contributes to perception of city as uncertain, dangerous

CONSEQUENCES/LIMITS

- social polarization?
- destruction of public space → uncertainty
- ↓ diversity/urban quality of life

Alternatives: Rogers, sustainable city?

Diagram G

In this section we are going to explore some of the second wave of changes and ask whether we are now living in an era of urban uncertainty – precisely how have politics and space been transformed? The role of the private sector and quango-led, market-driven urban redevelopment is considered in more detail in Section 4 which looks at the redevelopment of Cardiff Bay and its impact on the communities of Butetown.

3.4.1 Cars, shops and space

ACTIVITY 17

Make short notes on the reading below.

Ken Worpole: 'What went wrong?'

[...] the main pressures which have historically affected urban life most profoundly in the past two decades [are]:

- the domination of transport by the private car;

- the impact of the 'retail revolution';

- and the privatization of leisure. [...]

Traffic in towns

If the town centre is now back as the key site of the urban policy advocated here, what happened to nearly destroy this cornerstone of urban life, or, in the words of J.B. Priestley, why did so many broken eggs and so few omelettes emerge from urban redevelopment in post-war Britain?

Much blame has been wrongly attributed to the influential report *Traffic in Towns*, produced by Colin Buchanan for the Ministry of Transport (1963). Buchanan's report anticipated the dangers to traditional town environments by the growth of car ownership, but unfortunately only some of his recommendations were ever acted upon. Not only did the report recommend new urban roads, ring roads and bypasses, it also came out strongly in favour of local government control of car parking numbers, charges and locations, as well as an expanded system of 'good, cheap public transport', and a staggering of working hours to avoid the early morning and early evening traffic jams which made urban life so unpleasant. Many of the ring roads were built, effectively cutting off many town centres from their residential hinterlands, but the recommendations for the control of car usage by heavy parking charges, improved and cheaper public transport and a number of other measures came to nothing. The motor-industry lobby, ever powerful, lobbied for roads, cheap car parking and an end to subsidized public transport. Bus passenger traffic declined nationally from 42 per cent of all journeys in 1953 to just 8 per cent in 1983. The effects are evident in every town and city in Britain today.

The impact of the car on modern towns has for the most part been disastrous. Ring roads have created major psychological barriers to walking or cycling in and out of town centres even from residential areas only 10 minutes' walking distance from the centre. In Preston we talked to people living on housing estates only a few minutes' walk away from the town centre who would never consider walking because of the physical and psychological obstacle courses involved. Pedestrian underpasses, tunnels, steps, broken pavements, traffic lights programmed at busy junctions to allow no more than seven seconds for pedestrians to cross (and some which allow pedestrians no time at all), have created major barriers to walking, particularly for those with pushchairs or for the disabled.

The use of cars to travel even short distances to work has meant the giving over of large areas of town-centre land to daytime car parking; at night these open car parks become bleak and wind-swept wastelands. In Basingstoke, the town-centre sports centre found that customers within easy walking distance preferred to drive. Some residential areas in Basingstoke have no obvious walking route into town. Multi-storey car parks, again busy by day but mostly empty at night, have become the new dragons' lairs of urban folklore. In Southend a council officer asked quizzically why it was that so many people who used the swimming pools, gyms and sports centres to keep fit all arrived in cars, even from the neighbouring residential areas. In Middlesbrough a woman told us that people used cars to travel to the next street.

Both the Civic Trust and the Town and Country Planning Association (TCPA) have warned against the continuing despoliation of Britain's town and city centres by car traffic; in August 1990 the Civic Trust published an environmental audit of 50 British cities which found that traffic congestion was the major issue [...]

Walking in towns and cities has been undervalued and often ignored by planners. Most traffic research fails to statistically register walking as a form of transport, even though half the journeys made within towns are made on foot. The people who walk are, not surprisingly, those who probably most need some form of assisted transport – research has shown that young men walk least and old women and young children walk most. The use of the car is inversely related to the need for it! Although shopping is regarded as one of the great pleasures of contemporary culture, according to the National Consumer Council (1987), 'for many hundreds of thousands of consumers it is little short of a nightmare. They are the low income families, the single parent families, the elderly, the disabled and the non-car owners.' A survey in Milton Keynes showed that three-quarters of housewives do not have access to the family car during weekdays. [...]

Safety issues are also involved. Britain prides itself on its comparatively low car-accident rate, but this is for car-occupant safety only; compared with the rest of the European Community only Spain, Portugal and Greece have worse pedestrian fatality rates, and the UK has the highest rate for children. [...]

In Germany traffic calming has reduced pedestrian accidents to 5 per cent of their previous level, and in Copenhagen provision for cyclists has recently doubled to 9 per cent the number of journeys to work made by bicycle.

Patterns in urban mobility are changing fast. This is why we can no longer take the car-strangled city or town centre as a given; within a decade many towns, like Brighton and Oxford already, will have banned non-essential car traffic in the town centres. Where will the new urban dynamic come from? What will we do with the spaces left behind?

The retail revolution

The second major impact on town-centre usage in the post-war era was the phenomenal effect of the 'retail revolution' which swept through Britain in the 1970s and 1980s. The revolution involved widespread physical alterations to the built fabric of most towns and cities, and changes in local economic leverage, involving: pedestrianization of high streets; development of covered shopping centres; appropriation and ownership of town centres by pension funds and insurance companies; creation of closed, private spaces in town centres where public thoroughfares and pedestrian routes once used to be; escalation of town-centre rents so that only multiples could afford to be there; requirement for large-scale dedicated car parking space; growth of the financial services sector in high-street premises (building societies, cash-dispensing machines); decline of secondary shopping areas; decline of town-centre housing and residential accommodation; and finally the marginalization of town-centre districts where traditional facilities (libraries, museums, theatres) were sited, as shopping centres created new centres of critical mass elsewhere. The effects of this transformation of many town and city centres are still being lived through. [...]

Town centres have appeared to move from multifunctional areas (government and commercial administration, artisanal production, service industries, religious worship, civic buildings and public entertainment, housing) towards monofunctionalism (shopping). In the process of change from urban production and administration to consumption, Bell (1979) has argued, some of the political and ethical functions of urban civic life have been lost. Planning has responded to these changes rather than attempting to intervene in the process of city-building. Peter Buchanan (1988) has argued that 'British planning is predicated upon a desperately impoverished conceptual model of the city. In essence that model (when planning still had some life and credibility) was consumerist rather than civic.' Planning responded to the car, responded to the in-town and out-of-town shopping centre, rather than seeking to shape the urban mix. One of the people interviewed in Preston said: 'The town centre is planned on the basis that no one respectable is out at night.'

The sheer scale of the impact of retailing cannot be underestimated. Between 1965 and 1986 developers built 660 new shopping centres averaging 153,000 square feet, roughly one new centre for every 80,000 people, which means often more than one new centre in every medium-sized town. In 1967 there was only one superstore in Britain; by 1983 there were 289. In 1977 there were less than 40 DIY warehouses in Britain; by 1987 there were over 600. The year 1988 was a record year for retail park openings, with 45 schemes completed, providing 5,765,000 square feet of floorspace.

The locational effects in town centres of this proliferation of shopping centres have often been disastrous. In Swansea, the High Street has almost been abandoned as new shopping centres have opened to the south of the city, and the main public library and fine Glynn Vivian Art Gallery have been left stranded on the northern town-centre perimeter. In Luton the Arndale centre blocks all pedestrian routes through the town centre, as does the main shopping centre in Basingstoke; in both towns the main pedestrian route to the main BR station involves walking through the private property of the shopping centre. In Basildon the opening of the Eastgate Centre shifted the 'centre' of the town east and left the new Towngate Theatre, main library, town church and municipal buildings relatively isolated.

Apart from the environmental impact of the centres, the local economic impact has been felt, too. The success of the multiples has been at the expense of local retailing, service industries and even production. Only the multiples have been able to afford the rent in the new malls and high street locations and local firms have been driven out of business. Between 1960 and 1989 the multiples increased their share of the retailing sales from 33 per cent to 80 per cent, giving them the giant's share of the market and of the town centre.

It was rare to find in or near town-centre sites, specialist shops such as picture framers, craft and artists' materials, health-food shops, antiques, wine-making and home brewing, cycle shops, hobby shops, radio repairers, second-hand bookshops, and many of the other shops that reflect an active participation in leisure. In Truro most of the local traders who accounted for nearly 80 per cent of shops and stalls, have vanished from the city centre. In Southend people complained that it was no longer possible to buy a pint of milk in the High Street; in Basingstoke people said it was difficult to buy a tin of paint. There were many complaints that in the large retail chains, shop staff were untrained and were often selling products – cameras, hi-fi equipment, tools, sports equipment – that they neither knew about nor understood. [...]

Retailing in Bath has been the subject of much discussion, with a 41 per cent increase in retail floorspace in the city between 1975 and 1987. 'Luxury shopping, once merely one of a profusion of treats, has become the city's *raison d'être*,' wrote Frances Anderton (1989), 'Bath is an extreme beneficiary and victim of a market economy and retailing revolution that threaten to overrun the entire nation with useless, aka luxury goods, shops and leave a trail of urban erosion in their wake.' Most of Bath's established stores have gone, and the multiples now occupy 104 sites in the main trading streets, compared with only 24 independents. However, such was the vulnerability of this luxury retailing to trade winds, that the combination of the uniform business rate and a downturn in the economy meant that 80 town-centre shops closed in 1990.

The owners of the shopping malls often have no direct interest in retailing, and certainly not in the life of the towns they are located in, for the majority of owners are pension funds and insurance companies which have invested in retail property as part of a wider portfolio. The main shopping centre in Basingstoke is owned by the Prudential; in Reading it is owned by Legal & General; in Stirling by

Standard Life; in Preston the St George's shopping centre is owned by Legal & General and the Fishergate Centre by Charterhouse Securities; in Southend a local land developer, Southend Estates, was bought out by Higgs & Hill. Their interest in the towns their money is invested in is remote if not non-existent; it is a financial relationship only, and only questions of the long-term economic viability of town-centre retailing will bring these companies to the local civic table. As Michael Middleton (1987) noted: 'Although 20% of British pension funds are invested in property, their investment capacity has rarely been used for revitalisation.' In England and Wales at least, there is no longer any local or regional capital source, no Luton Bank or Bank of Swansea. In America and many West European countries, local and regional banks continue to play an important part in urban renewal.

We also noted the effects of multiple ownership of retailing on staff attitudes among shop workers, who now constitute one of the largest groups of workers in the town centre. Much modern retail work is part-time, low-paid, unskilled and often highly casualized. In Swansea, for example, where we looked at retail workers' conditions in detail, part-time jobs accounted for two-thirds of all retail employment, with 85 per cent of the staff of firms like Marks & Spencer part-time. Two-thirds of all retail jobs were held by women. In Preston 26% of all town-centre employment was made up of part-time women's jobs.

For shop workers, coming into the town centre every day was no different from going to work in a factory. We realized that if attitudes towards seeing the town centre as a lively, public site for leisure and recreation were to change, then town-centre workers could play a key role as 'ambassadors' for urban renewal. Making them aware of – and even giving them discounted access to – local cafés, restaurants, leisure centres, cinemas and theatres, would encourage a positive attitude towards the town centre rather than the negative one we often found.

The recession, together with increasing consumer resistance to 'sameness' in shopping centres, has sparked off a move back towards diversity. The famous Metro Centre in Gateshead, the largest self-contained out-of-town shopping mall in the UK to date, has put a ban on any further financial services companies taking shops because 'they don't give anything to the variety of the centre', and is seeking to include a post office, library and police station among new lettings. There is already a parish priest there. New local traders can start off by taking a barrow in the Metro Centre and, if successful, move into one of the proper shops. In Hounslow the Treaty Shopping Centre also contains a magnificent new public library which is as well used and popular as the Debenhams store next to it. [...]

The privatization of leisure

It has been argued that another key factor in the decline of town-centre vitality has been the increased privatization of leisure and the growth of domestic entertainment. This has been put most tellingly by the sociologist, Laurie Taylor [...], who has written: 'Today, the cinema and theatre have long since turned into the home video; the launderette and laundry into Ariston and

Hotpoint; the library into Penguin and Pan; the concert hall into a compact disc.' The sheer visual evidence of the growth of video hire shops, the annual statistics published showing the degree of penetration of television in British households and the average number of hours it is watched each week (25.5 hours a week per average viewer), of the takeaway food and drink trade figures, all seem to attest to an irreversible trend towards the domestication of free time, a trend also supported by the major investment in homes and the continued growth of owner-occupation.

That trend has been also exacerbated by the growth of suburbanization, of urban 'growth by civic depletion' as Lewis Mumford (1945) called it, describing the proliferation of housing areas without any public amenities at all. A Conservative MP Sir Gerald Vaughan described the growth of suburban housing in and around Reading as follows: 'We have thousands of unhappy people who have moved into new houses on these huge estates. They find they have no proper schools, no shops, many of the roads are unmade and there is no proper health cover ...'. The demand by developers to be allowed to build 'new villages' in South-East England has recently begun to be resisted by politicians and planners who fear for the green belt. Surely the real issue is to make existing towns and cities better places to live in?

We looked for, and found, evidence that pointed to contradictory patterns of free-time use. It was noted earlier that spending on physically active sports is slowly increasing, as is spending on eating out and going to the cinema. The growth of cinema admissions and the beginning of a downturn in video hire, the fact that half the eligible population visit a pub at least once a week, a quarter claim to eat out at least once a week, a quarter attend religious meetings, and 15 per cent of the population do voluntary work at least once a week, all suggested that people still led active lives, supported by statistics showing that there was no decline evident at all in participation in voluntary organizations, amateur music and drama clubs, and other self-organized groups. It can be argued that people still make effective choices in leisure and the majority still do go out quite frequently rather than stay at home 'glued to the television', as the popular stereotype has it.

The move from mass employment to smaller units, the growth of small business and self-employment, also contribute, we believe, to the possibilities of a renewed urban culture, as these forms of employment in themselves can regenerate urban areas through infill development, the transformation of redundant factories into managed workspaces, the growth of the services sector, bringing back into towns and cities new forms of production. The liberalization of 'use classes' in planning legislation can also be beneficial in mixing residential, light industry and retailing in or near town centres.

For the economic aspects of town-centre revitalization are of the greatest importance. Town-centre renewal can only come about if land-use planning is replaced by activity-based planning which works economically. [...]

A programme for new, more localized urban economies, has already been outlined by the economist, Robin Murray (1991), in a study based on successful developments in Germany and Italy. Strengthening local economic circulations, of goods and services produced locally, is essential if towns and cities are to be shielded from the global effects of markets acting arbitrarily. The traditional 'one-industry' town cannot survive in the future as the fate of many of the shipbuilding, steel, fishing or mining towns in the UK has demonstrated. Flexible specialization in manufacturing, and the growth of service economies, puts local trading back on the agenda again. Ecological politics also provides the incentive for recycling, energy conservation, and a 'make-and-mend' approach to goods and services rather than deskilled mass production and consumption.

References

Anderton, F. (1989) 'Shopping mad: the erosion of urbanity', *Architectural Review*, May.

Bell, D. (1979) *The Cultural Contradictions of Capitalism*, London, Heinemann.

Buchanan, P. (1988) 'What city? A plea for place in the public realm', *Architectural Review*, November.

Middleton, M. (1987) *Man Made the Town*, London, Bodley Head.

Ministry of Transport (1963) 'Traffic in towns: a study of the long term problems of traffic in urban areas', *Report of the Working Group* (Buchanan Report), London, HMSO.

Mumford, L. (1945) *The Culture of Cities*, London, Secker and Warburg.

Murray, R. (1991) *Local Space: Europe and the New Regionalism*, Centre for Local Economic Strategies, Manchester.

National Consumer Council (1987) Paper at National Chamber of Trade Conference (Janet Graham), 11 October.

Source: Worpole, 1992, pp.13–23

COMMENT

The key points of Worpole's argument that we noted were:

1 (a) ↑ of motor car – due to car industry, lobby, massive provision of infrastructure and parking but no charges (controls, public transport ↓) <u>cars dominate public space</u>.

   (b) → massive physical/mental barriers to walking/cycling, esp. for kids/disabled.

   (c) → inequality for those with no access to car.

   (d) → bad child safety.

2 retail revolution

   many new developments, shopping malls, out of town shopping

   town centre rents

   decline city centre amenities and accommodation

   shift: multi → mono functionalism of town centre

planning has supported this

→ empty town centres become dangerous (especially at night)

diminishing diversity

polarization as ↑ luxury shops ↓ secondary shopping centres.

3 privatization of leisure

cf. Laurie Taylor ↓ cinema, theatre, library, ↑ videos, TV, etc.

   → suburbanization and ↑ density ↓ amenities.

NB evidence against this – high levels of participation etc. still found.

So, Worpole is arguing that the decline of diverse, multi-functional, living city centres has been the key change in all cities recently. Combining with earlier trends, suburbanization and out-migration from big cities, intensified car use and retailing shifts have left old public spaces – perceived as dangerous and therefore empty – derelict and unused though there is some evidence to the contrary in some cities.

3.4.2 Crime

To conclude the discussion of uncertainty and diversity we return to the theme of the *Introductory Chapter*, the issue of crime. As we noted, the idea that crime is engulfing the UK, particularly the cities, giving rise to periodic moral panics, is by no means a recent feature in society. During the 1980s and 1990s, concerns about rising crime levels have been heightened by episodes of large-scale 'rioting' over racism and discrimination, oppressive policing and the poll tax. In the early 1980s and early 1990s riots in many UK cities were described by politicians from across the political spectrum, as well as some social scientists, as a sign of a wider 'disorder' or 'malaise' in UK society: areas of cities had, it seems, become 'dangerous places' (Campbell, 1993). Yet as Nick Fyfe points out, there are marked intra-urban variations in crime.

ACTIVITY 18

Study carefully the following extract from Fyfe's analysis of crime in Edinburgh in the early 1990s.

What are the key patterns of crime that emerge from this study?

Nick Fyfe: 'Crime and the quality of urban life'

Just as the risks of victimization vary over space, so too does the degree to which people see crime as a problem. In central Edinburgh, for example, less than 10 per cent of those asked thought crime was a major problem (Anderson *et al.* 1990: 11) whereas in Islington (an inner city area of London) over 80 per cent thought it was (Crawford *et al.* 1990: 22–3). Superimposed on these inter-urban differences are equally marked intra-urban variations. The ECS [Edinburgh Crime Survey] contrasted affluent, suburban Corstorphine, where about 5 per cent of respondents see crime as a big problem, with Craigmillar, the relatively poor council estate where the figure is over 70 per cent. As these figures suggest, anxiety about crime is closely associated with the real risks of victimization in an area, something confirmed by the results of the most recent British Crime Survey [BCS]. Table 10.5 shows clearly that those living in high crime risk areas, the inner city, and places where there are signs of 'disorder', such as vandalism and graffiti, are generally far more anxious about crime than those living elsewhere. Local crime surveys reinforce the findings from the BCS, as Figure 10.2 [overleaf], showing fear of crime in Edinburgh, illustrates. Those living in Craigmillar are not only more often victims of crime than those living in some other parts of the city but they also tend to be more worried about crime. Thus 'it is not only crime but fear of crime that is a problem for poor communities, where it both compounds and is compounded by other problems associated with deprivation' (Kinsey 1993: 32).

TABLE 10.5   Area of residence and anxiety about crime

	Feeling unsafe out at night (%)	Feeling unsafe at home (%)	Very worried about burglary (%)	Very worried about mugging (%)
Risk of crime in ACORN [a] *area:*				
High	41	15	26	23
Medium	39	13	24	23
Low	28	9	15	15
Area:				
Inner city	43	15	27	25
Non-inner city	30	10	17	16
Signs of disorder in area:				
More of a problem	41	15	25	23
Less of a problem	27	8	15	15
All BCS	32	11	19	18

[aACORN = A Classification of Residential Neighbourhoods which assigns respondents' homes to neighbourhood groups according to demographic, employment, and housing characteristics of the immediate area.]
Source: Mirrlees-Black and Maung 1994

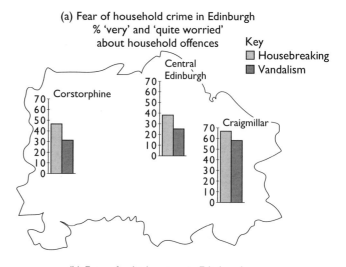

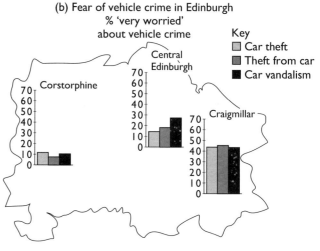

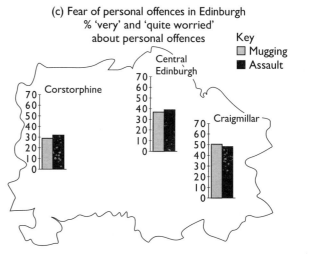

FIGURE 10.2   Fear of crime in Edinburgh

Source: Anderson *et al.* 1990

In making sense of these anxieties about crime, however, it is important to recognize that spatial variability in the fear of crime cannot be accounted for only by variations in the risks of crime. There are a variety of non-crime, place-based factors that also generate fear (Smith 1987). Indeed, several researchers have highlighted the relationship between fear and the urban landscape, focusing on how features of the 'situational' environment, comprising both physical and social elements, appear to prompt feelings of unsafety (Bannister 1991, 1993). These features include the run-down and vandalized appearance of a neighbourhood, poor street lighting, youths loitering and the perceived existence of places where potential assailants can hide. The presence and absence of these physical and social cues creates a dynamic mental map which defines those places that are safe and unsafe during the day and after dark. Such mental maps will, of course, be socially differentiated, with gender, age and household income all significant variables in understanding reactions to crime. Indeed, as Table 10.6 shows, there are clear variations between social groups in terms of the impact of crime on the spatial practices of everyday life.

TABLE 10.6 The impact of crime on daily life – precautions taken when out at night

	Ever avoid going out alone because of risks of crime (%)	Take car rather than walk (%)	Go out with someone else (%)	Avoid certain streets (%)
Total sample	26	23	18	26
Men	10	15	61	21
Women	37	30	29	30
16–24 years	19	18	25	35
25–44 years	23	28	19	29
45–64 years	25	22	16	22
65 and over	44	16	14	17
Under £10K	31	15	18	20
£10K to £19,999	19	30	17	29
£20K and over	16	43	15	42

Source: Kinsey and Anderson 1992

What stands out from this table is the extensive precautionary behaviour adopted by women in order to reduce their risks of victimization from crime and harassment. Nearly four times as many women as men avoid going out alone because of the risks of crime and twice as many take the car rather than walk as a precaution against crime at night. The restrictions on women's spatial behaviour resulting from the fear of crime are therefore severe. Research in inner city areas of London points to women living under a self-imposed curfew after dark as they avoid being alone in public space, avoid public transport and subways and, if they have to go out, often rely on men as escorts (Painter 1992). Moreover, it is women's fear of male sexual violence that particularly curtails their use of public space. As Valentine's (1989, 1992) study in Reading reveals, many of women's 'taken-for-granted' choices of routes and destinations are in fact the product of coping strategies that women adopt to stay safe, given their fears of sexual assault. The irony of these actions, however, is that statistically women are more likely to be assaulted at home by men they know than they are by strangers in public spaces. Explaining this 'spatial paradox', Pain's (1993, see too Pain 1991) interviews with women in Edinburgh indicate that it reflects partly the way in which women are brought up to be fearful of public space and partly women's experience of public places where they are routinely subject to sexual harassment but not assault. Furthermore, it is important to recognize that the large-scale withdrawal of women and, indeed, many men from public spaces after dark not only involves costs to these people themselves, in terms of foregoing social and leisure opportunities, but also has costs for the community more generally: the fewer people there are on the streets at night, the lower the possibility of intervention should a crime occur and the fewer the possible witnesses to incidents, thus increasing levels of anxiety among those who continue to use public spaces after dark.

Anxiety about crime, like crime itself, is thus not randomly distributed across society or over space but affects particular people living in particular places more than others. Moreover, the adaptation and reordering of the routines of everyday life prompted by the fear of crime indicate its negative impact on the quality of life of those living in the city.

References

Anderson, S., Smith, C.G., Kinsey, R. and Wood, J. (1990) *The Edinburgh Crime Survey: First Report*, Edinburgh: Scottish Office Central Research Unit.

Bannister, J. (1991) *The Impact of Environmental Design upon the Incidence and Type of Crime: A Literature Review*, Edinburgh: Scottish Office Central Research Unit.

— (1993) 'Locating fear: environment and ontological security' in H. Jones (ed.) *Crime and the Urban Environment: The Scottish Experience*, Aldershot: Avebury: 85–98.

Crawford, A., Jones, T., Woodhouse, T. and Young, J. (1990) *The Second Islington Crime Survey*, Middlesex University Centre for Criminology.

Kinsey, R. (1993) 'Crime, deprivation and the Scottish urban environment' in H. Jones (ed.) *Crime and the Urban Environment: The Scottish Experience*, Aldershot: Avebury: 15–44.

Kinsey, R. and Anderson, A. (1992) *Crime and the Quality of Life: Public Perceptions and Experiences of Crime in Scotland – Findings from the 1988 British Crime Survey*, Edinburgh: Scottish Office Central Research Unit.

Mirrlees-Black, C. and Maung, N.A. (1994) *Fear of Crime: Findings from the 1992 British Crime Survey*, London: Home Office Research and Statistics Department, Research Findings No. 9.

Pain, R. (1991) 'Space, sexual violence and social control: integrating geographical and feminist analyses of women's fear of crime', *Progress in Human Geography*, 15(4): 415–31.

— (1993) 'Women's fear of sexual violence: explaining the spatial paradox' in H. Jones (ed.) *Crime and the Urban Environment: The Scottish Experience*, Aldershot: Avebury: 55–68.

Painter, K. (1992) 'Different worlds: the spatial, temporal and social dimensions of female victimization' in D. Evans, N.R. Fyfe and D.T. Herbert (eds) *Crime, Policing and Place: Essays in Environmental Criminology*, London: Routledge: 164–95.

Smith, S.J. (1987) 'Fear of crime: beyond a geography of deviance', *Progress in Human Geography*, 11(1): 1–23.

Valentine, G. (1989) 'The geography of women's fear', *Area*, 21(4): 385–90.

— (1992) 'Images of danger: women's sources of information about the spatial distribution of male violence', *Area*, 24(1): 22–9.

Source: Fyfe, 1997, pp.251–5

C O M M E N T _____

The key points from Fyfe's study that we noted are:

1   There are significant variations between and within cities in how 'dangerous' and 'disordered' they are, how high the threat of crime is.

2   This is partly related to real risks and dangers, and partly a matter of perception; above all – the nature of urban landscapes (transformed as described in Worpole, Reading 8).

   see impact of this on different social groups in Table 10.6.

3   Note – vicious circle of:

   space perceived as dangerous → withdrawal of people → less witnesses/eyes on the street → space perceived as dangerous.

For Fyfe crime has major consequences for the quality of urban life, but also reflects wider changes in urban life. Contrary to much media reporting, the fear of crime and the experience of crime tends to be greatest among more disadvantaged and vulnerable groups: in the Edinburgh study this was highlighted in both housing estates and among women. However, crime, then, like the idea of a loss of community, can become the focal point for wider expressions of uncertainty and fear of the consequences of change:

> The spatial coalescence of crime with other social and economic ills means that people's experiences of the problems of crime compound and are compounded by other problems that may have nothing to do with crime itself, problems which may range from an inadequate bus service or poor street lighting to the social isolation of the elderly, or the simple feeling of yet another problem in an already difficult world.

(Fyfe, 1997, p.259)

3.5 Conclusion and summary

Our notes on both the Worpole and the Fyfe readings suggest that the uncertainties around urban living, its changes and discontents have multiple and complex origins. Moreover, there is both evidence to suggest that the degree of uncertainty is socially variable and can be misrepresented or misjudged, and that vicious circles of over-reaction and withdrawal can create self-fulfilling prophecies.

How can we begin to draw this together with the material in the rest of this section as well as earlier parts of DD100?

We have had a go at sorting your notes around our sceptical questions. You should have a look at these and amend and develop them with your own revision and synthesis.

1 Simple narratives of social change.

- Simple narratives of 'golden age' → social change → uncertainty and fragmentation have significant currency in popular culture.

- NB: how are these linked to moral panics and the creation of mythical pasts to deal with an uncertain present (see *Introductory Chapter*, Section 3.2 and TV 07 especially)?

  See also narratives of social change, risk and expert knowledge in Blocks 2 and 5; security of family, work and welfare in Block 3.

2 Was there ever a 'golden age'?

- Note contradictory evidence in the Introductory Block on crime; Block 3 on insecurities and conflict in traditional families, old labour markets, etc.

- Note simplicities and certainties, see Britishness (Book 1, Chapter 4 and TV 01) – always obscured inequalities between the 'nations' of the UK and aristocratic dominance of Englishness.

- Note traditionalist accounts of globalization challenge the idea that there was ever an era in which nation-states were disconnected from an uncertain global environment.

3 What have been the main forms of diversity emerging in the post-war UK?

- Increasing diversity and/or fragmentation in identities (class, gender, nation) in Block 1 and institutions in Block 3 (families, work).

- Increasing diversity of knowledge systems, especially medicine, Book 2, Chapter 2.

- Increasing diversity of cultures/peoples in global networks, Book 4, Chapter 2.

4　Has diversity been the only source of uncertainty? What else?

- Inequalities in power are an important source of uncertainty, especially in the labour market; fate of workers under globalization; gap between public and expert knowledge.

- Fundamental shifts in the structure of the economy – globalization/labour markets/emergence of knowledge economy and service industries, increasing environmental destructiveness (see, for example, Book 5, Chapter 4, Section 4).

- In the case of cities the dominance of market-driven, private-sector development, especially retail development, has been key; see account of welfare change in Book 3, Chapter 4.

- Technological change is also important: IT, cars, etc., but beware technological determinism.

5　Is the contemporary era necessarily worse? Are there benefits to diversity?

- See debate over multiculturalism and plural identities in Book 1, Chapters 1–4 on virtue of diversity. See also Book 3, Chapter 2 on the types of diversity amongst modern family forms; Book 4, Chapter 2 on the virtues of hybrid global cultures.

- See Book 5, Chapters 1 and 2 on the virtues of diversity in health beliefs and spiritual beliefs; and Book 5, Chapter 3 on the resilience of political ideologies.

- But *contra* this, see the account of diversity and uncertainty amongst post-modernists and advocates of the risk society, Book 5, Chapter 4, Sections 3 and 4.

4 STRUCTURE, AGENCY AND URBAN CHANGE

4.1 Revisiting structure and agency

Now to the second DD100 theme, *structure and agency*. By now you'll be aware that the relationship between structure and agency is a key issue in the social sciences. Broadly speaking the debate is about agents – which can be individuals or collectivities – and how they both are constrained by structures and, at the same time, reproduce structures. The debate reflects on the autonomy which we enjoy as individuals or collectivities to think and act as we choose; the constraints, the external pressures, which limit this freedom; and about how structures are reproduced through social action.

By now you've done a great deal of work on structure and agency. The first four blocks were summarized in the *Mid Course Review*, and you should take a chance now to quickly skim your own notes and thoughts on the subject. The summary diagram on structure and agency from the *Mid Course Review* is reproduced here as Figure 5.

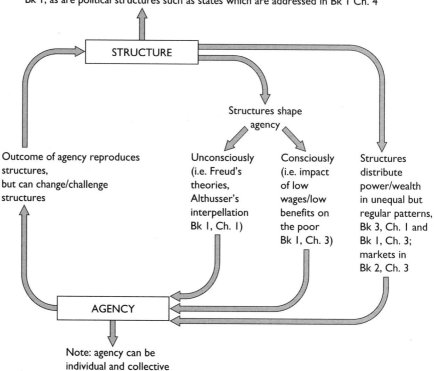

Structures come in a number of forms, for example biological, such as Darwinian arguments and the genetic shaping of intelligence (Bk 2, Ch. 1)
Economic structures are illustrated by the distribution of wealth, work and employment (as in Bk 1, Ch. 3)
Cultural factors, such as assumptions about gender and ethnicity, are discussed in Bk 1, as are political structures such as states which are addressed in Bk 1 Ch. 4

STRUCTURE

Structures shape agency

Outcome of agency reproduces structures, but can change/challenge structures

Unconsciously (i.e. Freud's theories, Althusser's interpellation Bk 1, Ch. 1)

Consciously (i.e. impact of low wages/low benefits on the poor Bk 1, Ch. 3)

Structures distribute power/wealth in unequal but regular patterns, Bk 3, Ch. 1 and Bk 1, Ch. 3; markets in Bk 2, Ch. 3

AGENCY

Note: agency can be individual and collective (see *Workbook 1*, Sect. 4.1)

FIGURE 5 Structure and agency: Introductory Block–Block 3, summary diagram

The Introductory Block introduced you to four different explanations of crime which focused on either individual agency or structural approaches (which look to broader social structures to explain crime). You encountered three different sorts of structure: the biological, the economic, and the cultural.

In Block 1 you examined the processes involved in identity formation, processes which are both individual and collective. On the one hand, it was clear that identities can be chosen and must be actively taken up by agents, but on the other hand the repertoire of roles and identities and possibilities that are available to us are clearly structured – in biological, geographical, economic, cultural, and political terms.

Block 2 began with an examination of various explanations of the origins of intelligence. In diverse ways, neo-Darwinian and different schools in psychology attribute differing significance to structure and agency, and the balance between these (see *Workbook 2*, Section 1.1). Similarly, Chapter 3 of Book 2 examined markets in terms of opportunities (for individual choice) and the constraints (of structures) which operate on this freedom. Moreover, the chapter argued that through the amalgamation of individual decisions and deductions, broader structures (such as the market) are reproduced.

Block 3 enriched our account of structure and agency by introducing the concepts of power, order and institutions into the debate. Let's pause for a moment to look at Block 3's account of power and its relationship to structure and agency (see Figure 6).

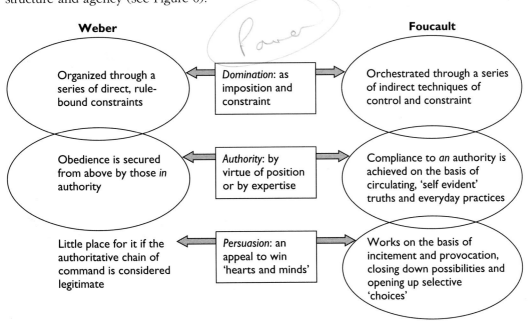

FIGURE 6   Two theories of power (Figure 1.8 from Book 3, Chapter 1)

Block 3 develops two broad theories of power – drawing on the work of Weber and Foucault. Both theories acknowledge different modes of power – domination, authority and persuasion – which draw on different kinds of structure and resources, but the theories deal with them differently, allot them different levels of importance and, as a consequence, deal with structure and agency differently. Drawing this together we came up with Table 6, which amalgamates our comments on Workbook Activities 1.5 and 1.6 in *Workbook 3*, p.69.

TABLE 6   Power, structure and agency

	Agency	Structure
Weber	Agents excise power. Agents' power comes from positions in organizations.	Structures determine the powers of agents. Structure disperses power and gives top-down control. Individuals as agents are heavily constrained by structures.
Foucault	Power works on and through agents. Anonymous forces (ideas, expectations) work on agents. By working with these forces agents themselves exercise power.	Structures constrain people by closing down other possibilities. Structures are produced by powerful agents negotiating power. Complex and changing networks as much as fixed structures shape power.

In Block 4 we saw that all structures – be they specific institutions or the patterns of social stratification such as the distribution of wealth – are spatially organized. Some structures are local, some national, some regional, and some global. Interestingly, as the focus of DD100 moved from the UK to the global arena, some of the things we described earlier as structures (the national market, an individual corporation or a nation-state) are now seen as agents; nation-states, for example, can be thought of as actors in the international system, and firms become agents in competitive global markets. So what is a structure and what is an agent is not always entirely clear. It depends on what it is that we are seeking to understand and what spatial level we are focusing on.

Finally, in Block 5, we examined how knowledge is a structure which shapes agency. Chapter 3 looked at political ideologies, and here you saw clearly how a body of knowledge shapes beliefs at the popular level, but is also used as a tool by politicians to achieve political change.

The structures which shape and influence the degree of agency people can exercise are based on a range of factors. These include economic, political, cultural, biological and environmental factors, and the material infrastructure of society. The form structures take includes patterns of social, economic stratification and specific institutions, and these operate at different spatial levels from the local to the global. Structural impact may operate at the level of the unconscious as well as shaping collective identities which form the basis of collective agency. The unequal distribution of wealth, power and cultural resources provides levels of constraint as well as the possibility of agency. Individual and collective agency reproduce, but also challenge, change and create new structures.

In this section of the *End of Course Review* we'll be tying together your work on structure and agency. Following our focus on cities, we'll be doing this by examining a case study of one city in the UK, Cardiff, the capital of Wales. In particular, we'll be looking at the redevelopment of Cardiff Bay, and we'll explore how notions of structure and agency are helpful for making sense of this example of contemporary social change in the UK.

In Section 4.2 we provide an outline history of development of Cardiff and in particular an area at the heart of Cardiff called Butetown. In Section 4.3 we begin to explore the *structures* which shaped the redevelopment of Butetown in the 1990s, while in Section 4.4 we look at how the agency of both formal and informal institutions in Cardiff and Butetown have resisted and reshaped those structures. In Section 4.5 we draw these threads together with a review of earlier materials in the course.

Before we turn to Cardiff, stop for a moment to think of any material or arguments that you covered in Section 2 of the *End of Course Review* which illuminate the structure and agency debate and, specifically, the process of urban redevelopment.

4.2 Setting the scene: Cardiff and Cardiff Bay

Cardiff is a fairly new city, and really played no significant role in the history of Wales prior to the nineteenth century. From under 2,000 in 1801, its population grew to 18,000 in 1851 and 164,000 by 1901. It grew one hundredfold between 1801 and 1911, faster than any other major town in the UK except Middlesbrough (Daunton, 1977). This nineteenth-century growth was based first on iron and then on coal. Crucial to the growth of Cardiff was the opening of the Glamorgan Canal in 1794, which linked Merthyr Tydfil with Cardiff. This was followed by the Taff Vale Railway in 1840 and the opening of the various docks in Cardiff between 1839 and 1907. Central to all of this was the entrepreneurial aristocrat, the Marquis of

Bute, on whose land much of the development occurred. Coal exporting
generated various ancillary industries, notably the railways, engineering,
steel, and shiprepairing, but Cardiff is unusual as a Victorian city in that it
never developed an indigenous manufacturing industrial base, mainly
because it had no pre-nineteenth century industry on which to base it.
At its peak (in 1912) Cardiff docks handled more cargo than London docks,
most of it Welsh steam coal which was exported to bunkering stations
throughout the British Empire. Cardiff, it was written in the *Cardiff Times*
in 1905,

> gave an impression of modernity and progressiveness, of spacious streets and
> buildings, of docks and ships, and of great commercial activity which well merit
> the epithet 'the Chicago of Wales' [...] It is both ancient and modern, Celtic and
> cosmopolitan; progressive; wealthy; enterprising; and a centre of learning. There
> is a Metropolitan ring about its large ideas and 'go' which makes all other Welsh
> towns seem parochial in comparison.
>
> (cited by Daunton, 1977, p.229)

All this was to change with the decline of the docks, beginning before the
First World War and finishing with the ending of coal exporting in 1964.

As the coal and associated industries have shrunk, Cardiff has developed
with a service sector dominated by administration, commerce, and shopping.
It has a population of about 300,000 with an employment pattern shown in
Table 7.

ACTIVITY 19

You should read Table 7 carefully and write about four short sentences which
summarize the key features of the nature and changes of employment in Cardiff
between 1981 and 1991.

TABLE 7 Percentage and net change in employment in Cardiff by sector and sub-sector 1981–91, by travel to work area

	Percentage change	Net change
Divisions		
Agriculture	−25.7	−197
Energy	−23.1	−1,463
Extraction	−34.6	−2,833
Metal goods	−11.5	−1,328
Other manufacturing	5.8	640
Construction	−15.7	−1,623
Distribution	11.5	3,804
Transport	24.8	3,645
Banking and finance	47.5	7,432
Others	11.7	7,556
Total	4.7	8,343
Classes		
Finance sub-sectors	37.6	1,521
Insurance	22.5	524
Business services	68.8	4,937
Renting of moveables	−25.6	−333
Real estate	98.1	783
Total	47.5	7,432
Public administration	9.5	1,727
Sanitary services	85.4	2,715
Education	−7.1	−1,040
R & D	34.5	114
Medical	−2.9	−430
Other public services	70.4	4,086
Recreation	8.2	508
Personal services	−8.8	−124
Total	11.7	7,556

Source: Census of Employment; cited by Gripaios *et al.*, 1997, p.586

COMMENT

We're not sure what sanitary services are, or why they have grown by 85 per cent in a decade! But we've noted:

- Agriculture, energy and extraction (that includes quarrying and mining) down about 25 per cent.

- Significant rises in banking and finance, transport and distribution.

- Very large growth of recreation, finance, business services and real estate employment.

- Huge growth of public services.

So this kind of employment change suggests Cardiff is a particular version of the post-industrial city (Book 5, Chapter 4, Section 2.1) in which public administration, rather than say business or industry, is the lead sector.

Why has this shift occurred? The capital status of Cardiff has been crucial in generating new jobs and investment. Cardiff has been the capital of Wales since 1955, seat of the Welsh Office since 1964, and home of the National Assembly for Wales since 1999. As a city, however, it has always enjoyed an ambivalent relationship with the rest of Wales. Historically, Cardiff's coal and shipowners were not local, and Cardiff as a place was incidental to the owners of its wealth. Many had been in business elsewhere, for example, John Cory had been a shipowner in Padstow.

> Coalowners lived outside Cardiff, their investments were in the coalfield and in coaling stations throughout the world [...] The 'legitimate' middlemen in coal had worldwide investments and were often part of national rather purely local concerns [...] The shipowners were similarly distant from the local society [...] these men were in but not of Cardiff, they had an office there but no real economic interest. It would not particularly have harmed these men if Cardiff did become a 'ruin as literally and lamentably as Carthage of old'. To them Cardiff docks were indeed no more than 'a convenience and economical means of carrying on their business'.

(Daunton, 1977, p.155)

More often than not owners' real economic interests and political concerns lay across the border in England. But as well as being closely linked with England, Cardiff has always enjoyed an ambivalent relationship with the rest of Wales and with the national movement in Wales – Cardiff's sense of self-sufficient, civic pride and cosmopolitanism has been somewhat removed from the rural culture and politics which has shaped Welsh nationalism. This gulf is reflected in the patterns of language use and in voting behaviour. A fifth of the population of Wales read, speak or write Welsh, but in South Glamorgan (Cardiff and the Vale of Glamorgan) the figure is 6 per cent.

Similarly, although the seat of the Welsh Assembly, Cardiff voted against devolution for Wales. Yet for over a century Cardiff increasingly played its hand as a capital city, and has enhanced considerably its administrative role and power in the process.

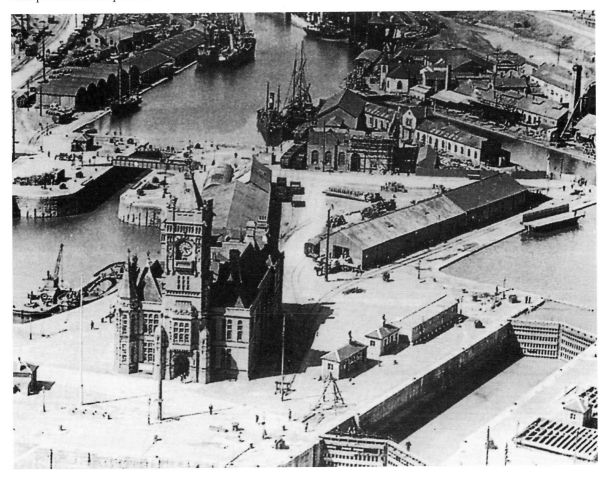

FIGURE 7   Victorian Pierhead building, Cardiff Bay

ACTIVITY 20

Take a look at Figures 8 and 9. What patterns do you see? What do they tell you about the spatial distribution of support for devolution?

If you know Wales in social, cultural, economic or political terms, what do they tell you about Wales?

From your work on Scottish nationalism (Book 1, Chapter 4), how does Wales seem to differ from Scotland?

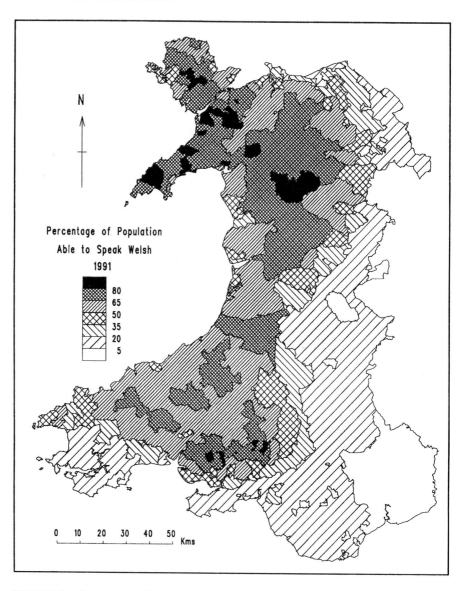

FIGURE 8   Percentage of the population able to speak Welsh, 1991

Source: Aitchison and Carter, 2000, p.95

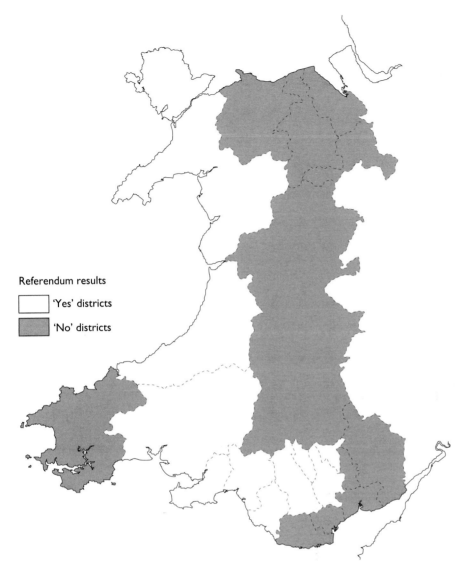

FIGURE 9 The Wales devolution referendum results, September 1997
Source: O'Leary, 1998, p.10

C O M M E N T

Clearly the constituencies where the 'no' votes predominated are mainly those adjacent to England – from the Vale of Glamorgan and Cardiff east to Monmouth, north through Powys, to north-east Wales, plus South Pembrokeshire, which is commonly known as 'little England beyond Wales'. These are precisely those areas where the proportion of the population able to speak Welsh is lowest – suggesting an English/Welsh divide in the devolution vote and a lack of support for devolution from Anglicized parts of Wales. This is rather deceptive, though, because about 40 per cent of the 'yes' votes were cast in 'no' constituencies, and plenty of the 'no' constituencies had larger 'yes' votes than some 'yes' constituencies. Moreover, there is some evidence of the vast variations within as well as between constituencies: in Cardiff one ward seems to have voted 20 per cent 'yes', while another was 90 per cent 'yes' (Trystan, 1997). So the maps in Figures 8 and 9 represent a very particular version of the data.

This is one example of the considerable diversity in Cardiff. In some ways the most distinct area of Cardiff is Butetown. Butetown is named after the Marquis of Bute who had been a key player in developing Cardiff and its docks. The family sold up, gave Cardiff Castle and Bute Park to Cardiff Corporation and moved back to the Isle of Bute (in Scotland) in 1948. Butetown is a small area – about a mile by a quarter of a mile – with clearly defined boundaries: the Glamorgan Canal, now filled in and grassed over, runs up the west side; a railway on an embankment defines the eastern border; the docks and sea lie to the south; and Butetown is separated from the city centre by the Paddington–Swansea railway line on an embankment in the north. The southern part of Butetown is referred to as 'the Docks' and the northern part as 'the Bay'. The whole area has been immortalized as 'Tiger Bay', by Shirley Bassey in particular.

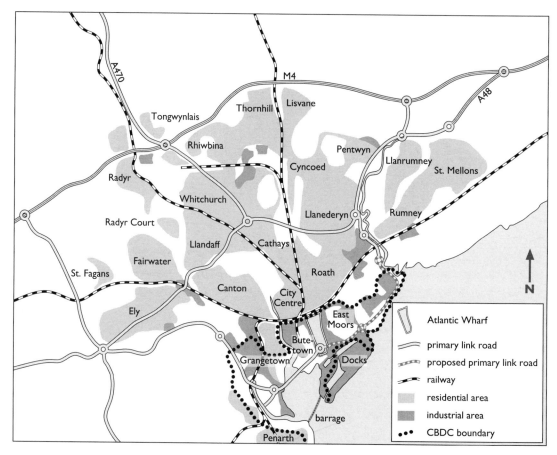

FIGURE 10   Map of Cardiff (CBDC is the Cardiff Bay Development Corporation)

Source: Thomas, 1992, p.84

Cardiff, like many other cities, is clearly structured in terms of 'race'. Cardiff has one of the oldest and longest established **black and minority ethnic group populations** in the UK, comprising 7 per cent of the population of Cardiff. The black and minority ethnic group population is most concentrated in Butetown, where the resident population is made up as shown in Table 8.

TABLE 8   Ethnic composition of Butetown, Cardiff, 1991

	%
White	60.3
Black groups	24.5
Indian/Pakistani/Bangladeshi	4.9
Chinese and other groups	10.2

Source: 1991 Census

However, these data and the census categories in Table 8 mask an even greater diversity. Within the small area of Butetown – which has never had a population of more than about 10,000 and which today numbers about 4,000 – is to be found the most remarkable mix of ethnic groups. Glenn Jordan, a North American anthropologist who studies Butetown, has listed the following as represented in Butetown in the past 150 years:

> Irish, Welsh, English, Scots, Turks, Cypriots, French, French-speaking West Indians (presumably from Martinique and/or Guadeloupe), Jamaicans, Barbadians, Trinidadians, Guyanese, British Hondurans, Panamanians, Bahamians, St Lucians, St Kittsians, Germans, Spanish, Portuguese, Cape Verdeans, Maltese, Italians, Chinese, Japanese, Malays, Indians (that is, people from what is now Pakistan, India and Bangladesh), Somalis, Yemeni, Egyptians, Jews, Poles, Estonians, Latvians, Ukrainians, Norwegians, Finns, Danes, Mauritians, Sierra Leoneans, Liberians, Nigerians, Cameroonians, Gambians, Ghanaians, Angolans, South Africans, North Americans and a few others (for example, one Maori and at least one Fijian). [...] Nearly all of the immigrants to Cardiff docklands were male – and virtually all of them settled in the Butetown area. Once there, they met and often married women from the South Wales valleys and other parts of the British Isles. Today, most of Butetown's residents (and former residents) are of 'mixed' ethnic heritage. It is very common to find families from the area that are Muslim and Christian and Black and White: indeed such families are far more common than ones that are only one race or only one religion. One well-known family is of West Indian, West European and Chinese origin; the origins of another are Somali (Sunni Muslim) and Russian Jewish. Nobody who is from Butetown finds this 'odd': it is only outsiders who do. [...] This is a genuinely cosmopolitan community, inordinately rich in culture – and, crucially, in cross-cultural and inter-racial understanding.

(Jordan and Weedon, 1995, pp.135–6)

So Butetown provides clear evidence to counter the myths of Welsh cultural homogeneity, or that the black British are a recent phenomenon. More than

Black and minority ethnic groups
Social scientists often include black and minority ethnic in their descriptions; 'black' is used to retain the political dimension of 'race' but is not a satisfactory classification for all minority ethnic people, so we use both (see also *Mid Course Review*, p.7).

this, the culture of Butetown runs against stereotypical representations of Wales; it's a far cry from eisteddfodau, leeks, miners, male voice choirs, and the Welsh language. In Butetown one finds large numbers of people who see themselves as both black and Welsh (although only 3 per cent of people in Butetown speak, read or write Welsh, compared with 6.5 per cent for South Glamorgan as a whole). There have been considerable tensions between various groups in Butetown and systematic discrimination against many of its inhabitants, with several race riots, notably in 1848 and in 1919. Today, however, Butetown is seen by many as a powerful example of inter-racial harmony. This cohesiveness developed in the inter-war period, and has been fostered by the physical and cultural isolation experienced by Butetown and its residents which continues today. Such isolation and the distinct nature of the community has meant that Butetown has always had its own internal organizations and networks.

> The people of the Bay formed many kinds of associations to defend themselves, to struggle against injustice and inequality, to rally to the aid of colonial causes, and to provide for their own social and spiritual needs. Ethnic groups, language groups and religious groups came together to worship and for support and solidarity and social intercourse. One group, The Sons of Africa, still exists [...] However disparate these many groups were, whenever the community felt itself under attack, they united for defence and counter-attack.
>
> (Sherwood, 1991, p.58)

By comparison to these internal structures and self images of normality, solidarity and harmony, Jordan and others have argued that the dominant external images and narratives of Butetown have been either dangerous (the squalor, disease, immorality, violence and filth) or romantic (the exotic 'other', the Mecca of racial harmony). The novelist Howard Spring summarized this in a much-quoted passage from his autobiography *Heaven Lies About Us*:

> There was a fascination in the walk through Tiger Bay. Chinks and Dagos, Lascars and Levantines slippered about the faintly evil by-ways that ran off from Bute Street. The whole place was a warren of seamen's boarding houses, dubious hotels, ships' chandlers smelling of rope and tarpaulin [...] It was a dirty, smelly, rotten and romantic district, an offence and an inspiration, and I loved it.
>
> (quoted in Evans *et al.*, 1984, p.44)

Both dangerous and romantic discourses can be seen as manifestation and cause of the exclusion of Butetown people from mainstream political and economic life in Cardiff.

> There have been, literally, thousands of newspaper articles (of which hundreds are feature articles). There have also been about ten novels and collections of short stories, a dozen or so television programmes, perhaps a few dozen radio programmes, hundreds of undergraduate projects and dissertations, a few dozen masters and doctoral theses, several plays and a feature film. [...] So,

ultimately, it is impossible to separate Tiger Bay from stories about it. Tiger Bay is a textual phenomenon – a set of related images and discourses – as much as it is a physical and social one.

(Jordan and Weedon, 1995, p.138)

The message has been a persistent one. Butetown is somewhere not to go, not for respectable society, or it is somewhere you can only go at the peril of your own safety. Although a textual phenomenon, data on Butetown, notably from the 1991 Census, indicate that its distinctiveness from the rest of Cardiff has a material basis. Butetown has the worst rate of unemployment in the old South Glamorgan area; 25 per cent in Butetown compared with 10 per cent for South Glamorgan as a whole. Butetown has about the highest rate in the County of South Glamorgan of persons with long-term illness (21%, compared with a county average of 14%). It has the lowest proportion of owner occupation (32%, compared with a county average of 71%) and about the highest proportion of local authority owned housing (47% of dwellings). It has the highest proportion of households with no car (66%, compared with a county average of 35%). It has more than double the county average number of single parent households, and is the area with the second highest proportion of single person households. Butetown can also be compared with Cardiff in terms of the occupation of its residents or, at least, the 75 per cent who were economically active.

ACTIVITY 21

Take a look at Tables 9 and 10. What are the key differences between Cardiff and Butetown?

TABLE 9 Occupation, Cardiff and Butetown, % of employees and self-employed, 1991

Occupation	Cardiff	Butetown
Managers and administrators	14.4	7.1
Professional occupations	11.2	6.1
Associated professional/technical	10.2	8.2
Clerical/secretarial	19.2	13.3
Craft and related	11.3	14.3
Personal/protective services	9.2	12.2
Sales occupations	7.6	9.2
Plant and machine operatives	7.8	11.2
Other occupations	8.4	17.3
Inadequately described	0.7	1.0

Source: 1991 Census

TABLE 10   Social class (% of residents age 16+), Cardiff and Butetown, 1991

Social class	Cardiff	Butetown
I Professional occupations	6.4	4.4
II Managerial and technical	27.4	15.9
III(N) Skilled occupations – non-manual	25.8	20.4
III(M) Skilled occupations – manual	19.1	21.2
IV Partly skilled occupations	13.0	23.0
V Unskilled occupations	5.7	8.8
Armed forces	0.3	0.9
On a government scheme	1.5	4.4
Inadequately described	0.9	0.9

Source: 1991 Census

Turning to patterns of crime, we can see clear structured differences. Butetown is near the top of the table of crime rates for Cardiff police sector; for example, with 191 burglaries per 100,000 population in 1997/98. Data on arrests (for all crimes) by ward of residence of people aged 10–17 likewise puts Butetown not in top place but very near the top of the table for Cardiff as a whole. Regarding racially motivated violence or harassment, however, Butetown is not a high crime area: it is not among the twelve wards in Cardiff which experienced five or more such incidents between 1996 and 1998.

In sum, there are considerable data to suggest massive and structured inequalities – which, as we saw in Book 1, Chapter 3, has significant consequences for agency.

In the last two decades Butetown has become the focus of a major state-sponsored scheme to redevelop Cardiff's docks and waterfront areas long-abandoned by the coal export industry and create what has become known as Cardiff Bay. Cardiff Bay – as we shall see – is a term which was created by the Cardiff Bay Development Corporation (CBDC), a government quango which was established in 1987 (and dissolved in 2000) to co-ordinate the redevelopment of 2,700 acres of Cardiff dockland. Designed to link Cardiff with its waterfront, Cardiff Bay redevelopment was modelled on similar waterfront regeneration schemes, notably Baltimore in the USA. The CBDC embarked on a massive programme of public expenditure – compulsorily purchasing land, installing roads and services and, crucially, marketing Cardiff Bay – to regenerate the city and its docks area. The CBDC claims to have attracted £1 billion of private sector investment, built 3,000 houses and created 12,500 permanent jobs – something under half of its target in each case although the figure masks the many jobs lost as the CBDC cleared away old industries (CBDC, 1999). The development includes the National Assembly building; a 5-star Forte hotel; a waterfront retail complex which creates a 'Covent Garden style' mix on the Bay's edge; a leisure and entertainment complex; and, most centrally, the 1.1 km Cardiff Bay barrage, which has created a freshwater lake of 50 ha in what was the estuary of the Rivers Taff and Ely. Let's examine this massive redevelopment scheme in terms of structure and agency.

4.3 Structure

There's a range of structures which can be seen as constituting a framework within which the Cardiff Bay redevelopment is taking place. Thinking about them spatially, we can see them as global, UK, Welsh and local structures, and we shall explore each briefly in turn.

First, the global. As we've said, Cardiff achieved global importance as the 'coal metropolis of the world'. Cardiff Coal Exchange was the hub of the coal export trade, which from the 1880s was dominated by South Wales. In other words, Cardiff's very existence as a city is rooted in the global coal trade. This trade largely fed the demands of ocean-going steamships for coal. The expansion of the cargo fleets, in turn, depended on free trade and the British Empire. The Cardiff bourgeoisie, the coalowners and shipowners, had no special interest in Cardiff; their involvement was a response to the UK and global coal market. So it's easy to see the South Wales and Cardiff economy for over a century as an integral part of the global economy. In recent years global connections have continued to be highly significant with nearly 400 overseas companies operating in Wales. This includes a relatively high level of Japanese companies (for example, Sony and Hitachi) which have established European manufacturing plants in South Wales. To a large degree such global locational decisions are beyond the control of nation-states.

Another driver of change in Cardiff has been its growth as a regional retailing centre (see Reading 8 above). This, again, reflects a broader, global trend in developed economies. Finally, to understand Cardiff Bay Development Corporation's scheme to reunite Cardiff with its waterfront, the global marketplace for investment is an important consideration: the mission of the Corporation was to 'put Cardiff on the international map as a superlative maritime city, which will stand comparison with any such city in the world' (CBDC, 1999). Huw Thomas, a town planner who is researching Cardiff Bay, argues that Cardiff, having established itself as the capital of Wales in demographic, commercial, social and cultural terms, is now, with the Bay redevelopment, set to join the wider, global stage. Thus, what lies behind not just the growth of Cardiff in the nineteenth century but also its redevelopment today are global economic networks.

The global economy, however, is not the only structure involved. The UK government, too, is responsible for a raft of legislation and policies which have constrained and shaped what happens in Cardiff Bay. Much of this regional economic policy or environmental legislation is formulated at the European level, or within a European framework. Other elements are more autonomous of the EU. Let's take two examples of significant UK state structures and policies: **quangos** and **privatization**. The growth of quangos under the Conservative governments of the 1980s and 1990s was crucial. The CBDC was an urban development corporation (UDC). UDCs were set up by a Conservative government to overcome the image problem of derelict areas and to transform inner cities, in specific locations, with significant powers over planning infrastructure and so on. Key to their modus operandi was that they were a public–private partnership and that they were outside local government control. The Board of Cardiff Bay Development Corporation, unlike UDCs in England, included some local authority representation, but was composed essentially of nominees of the Secretary of State for Wales. The main private sector partner in the regeneration was Associated British Ports (ABP), owner of 60 ha of prime, waterfront land. ABP, formed when the British Transport Docks Board was privatized in the 1980s, entered into an agreement with the CBDC to collaborate in promoting the development and sharing the benefits. So there was in place a private organization with which the CBDC, the government quango, had to collaborate. In other words, the public sector – although in the case of Cardiff Bay very much holding the upper hand – had to formulate and implement its plans and share the benefits in ways which met the interests of the main private landowner.

Moving down from the national/UK level we can identify some key structures at the level of Wales. To make sense of economic regeneration in Wales generally, and Cardiff Bay in particular, one has to take account of the cohesiveness of Wales and its distinct political institutions. With a Minister in the Cabinet and its own well-funded economic development agency, the Welsh Development Agency, Wales is said by some to have achieved more co-ordinated and better funded economic development than much of the rest of the UK. A common complaint of the English regions is their disadvantaged position relative to that of Wales in terms of the incentives they are able to offer potential inward investors. Within Wales the development of Cardiff as a capital city has been central to the city's growth and this in turn has shaped the process of redeveloping Cardiff Bay. The EU Summit in 1998 and the Rugby World Cup in 1999 cemented the city's capital status but, most important, was devolution and the establishment of the National Assembly for Wales in 1999. Although an extremely close vote – with a 50.3 per cent turnout and only 50.3 per cent of these voting in favour – it was the Assembly which proved the turning

Quangos
Quasi-autonomous non-governmental organizations.

Privatization
The transfer of state assets or service provision to the private sector.

point for the Cardiff Bay scheme. It was only after this that flats were first sold for over £300,000 and that the area finally developed a highly attractive and up-market image.

At a more local level, the city council and Cardiff's particular sense of civic pride have helped to structure the development. Cardiff's urban identity grew out of the conflict between Liberal councillors and the Marquis of Bute and his estate in the nineteenth century, in which the Marquis' hegemony was challenged successfully. In this struggle between public and private, the public sector was victorious. Cardiff's strong public civic identity is manifest in the quasi-colonial buildings of the Civic Centre in Cathays Park which were finished just after Cardiff became a city in 1905. The Town Hall and Law Courts were opened in 1906–07, at which time the *Cardiff Times* commented:

> Cardiff has always been eager to take its proper place in the Principality as in the country in which it is situated, and has not failed to do its duty in national and international affairs. It is known the world over as the greatest coal port [...] The palaces erected in Cathays Park crown its recognition of civic duty and sacrifice which was recognised when the town was made a city, and it is hoped that its recognition as the natural centre in the county for affairs of government and intellectual life will follow.
>
> (cited by Evans, 1985, pp.382–3)

Through its struggle with the Marquis of Bute, the middle class strengthened its identity and confidence. One commentator described this in 1905 as follows:

> Its wide, well-paved, clean, electrically-lighted streets, through which runs one of the finest equipped systems of electric cars in the kingdom together with its fine business premises, stamps it out at once as a town of importance, and of wealth and prosperity. Its public institutions, its Free Library, College, Infirmary, Parks and open spaces tell of the spirit in which public undertakings have been approached, whilst the Town Hall and the Law Courts and the Cathays Park, where will be also erected the College, the Intermediate School and nearby the New Theatre, all indicate a large and public-spirited policy which has been pursued by the ratepayers.
>
> (cited by Evans, 1985, p.374)

With this strong sense of public pride and the long-term influence of state bodies on the city's development, private sector interests have tended to be relatively subordinate.

FIGURE 11   Cathays Park: Law Courts, City Hall and National Museum, c.1950

A photograph of Cathays Park is shown in Figure 11. In what sense do these buildings befit a city which was playing a significant role in the global economy in 1906?

How are they appropriate for Cardiff's more recent role as a capital city?

To sum up the various levels of institutions and politics: Cardiff Bay redevelopment took place and took the form that it did as a result of intersecting structures at various levels – local (Cardiff), national (Wales), national (UK), European, and global. At the heart of this was public–private partnership: the various state bodies worked in close collaboration with, in particular, the major landowner. Although set up by a Conservative government to bypass local democracy and to work with the private sector, the CBDC was expected to achieve its objectives by working with a diversity of other bodies, rather than undertaking the development itself. Nor, of course, were these various bodies working entirely in harmony, or with identical interests.

These government agencies and their policies are not the only relevant structures. Amongst the host of other individuals, collectivities and institutions which have been involved is the local press. As is common, the local press supported the local authority's policies of redevelopment, which were presented as contributing to Cardiff's civic standing. With no apparent irony, the *Western Mail* actively supported the government's vision of Cardiff as 'one of Europe's premier cities' (*Western Mail*, 1993). 'The local press was unashamedly promoting redevelopment and was not interested in residents' views; there was de facto exclusion of their views, and voices' (Thomas *et al.*, 1996, p.190). In its content and headlines the local press acted as an unpaid public relations machine for the CBDC.

To summarize this sub-section we have tried to pull together the threads of the argument in diagrammatic form and we've added some links to other parts of the review, see Diagram H(a) and (b). This is our example of making notes on this material which you can look at. You may prefer to make your own notes in another form of course. You should use the form with which you feel happiest for your own notes.

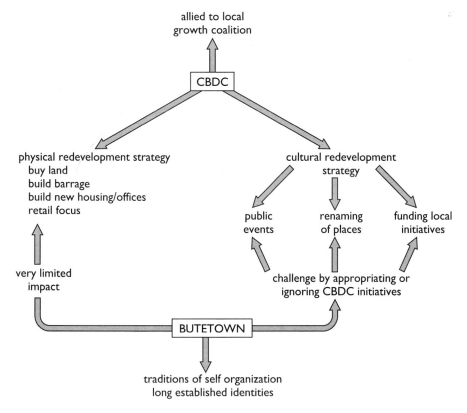

Diagram H(a)

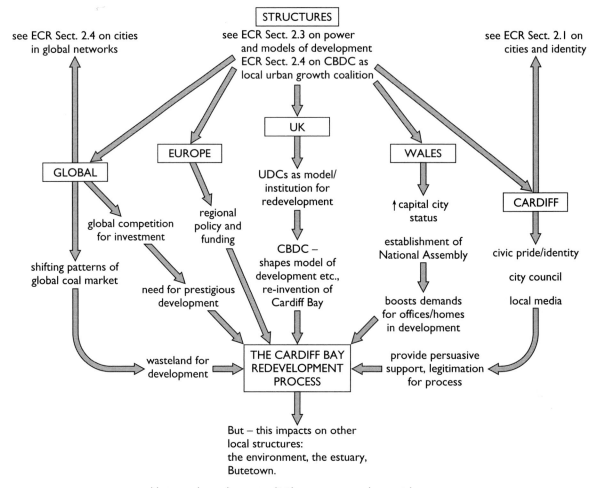

Diagram H(b)

The diagram contains the following text:

STRUCTURES

see ECR Sect. 2.4 on cities in global networks

see ECR Sect. 2.3 on power and models of development
ECR Sect. 2.4 on CBDC as local urban growth coalition

see ECR Sect. 2.1 on cities and identity

UK

EUROPE

WALES

GLOBAL

CARDIFF

global competition for investment

regional policy and funding

UDCs as model/ institution for redevelopment

↑ capital city status

shifting patterns of global coal market

need for prestigious development

CBDC – shapes model of development etc., re-invention of Cardiff Bay

establishment of National Assembly

civic pride/identity

city council

local media

boosts demands for offices/homes in development

wasteland for development

THE CARDIFF BAY REDEVELOPMENT PROCESS

provide persuasive support, legitimation for process

But – this impacts on other local structures: the environment, the estuary, Butetown.

Note: we have chosen to divide up structures by spatial level – how might we think about this in terms of forms of structure (institutions, social stratification) or types of structure (biological, cultural, economic, etc.)?

4.4 Agency

These large-scale and powerful institutions of Cardiff's urban growth coalition are not the end of the story. They were important, but their authority and power was not unlimited or unconstrained. For the redevelopment of Cardiff Bay to take place, they had to develop some sort of legitimacy in the eyes of those most affected. As is commonly the case, the scope for coercion (although it existed and was used in the form of compulsory purchase orders) was circumscribed. Persuasion, cajoling and working with others – albeit in a structured context – were more important. The CBDC and its allies had to mould individuals' and groups' beliefs and actions.

Central to the CBDC's redevelopment aim was to construct a balanced community. Given the racial, social and income characteristics of the Butetown population, this meant attracting white people of higher social classes, with higher incomes. The CBDC had to make (potential) newcomers and visitors to the Bay feel comfortable – which they would not in Butetown as it had existed hitherto. As the tone of the neighbourhood is changed, the 4,000 indigenous people of Butetown, by definition, become more marginal in setting the ambience of the area.

Changing the meaning of Butetown by changing perceptions of the docks area was a central task facing the CBDC. Indeed, it was the key to the process of modernization. For investment to be attracted the image of the area had to change, from the dangerous and exotic to the modern and desirable. Now, this is easier said than done because, as the cultural geographer Linda McDowell (1994) has argued, senses of place are often constructed by the powerless, rather than the powerful. Local residents, generally speaking, have not been supportive of the CBDC, and particularly so regarding the Cardiff Bay barrage element of the redevelopment. In many parts of Cardiff there were fears of damage to property as a result of the rise in groundwater level that the barrage scheme necessitates. In Butetown, however, the perceived threat has been more substantial than this – the attempted obliteration of, or at least profound changes to, their identity. The strength and depth of local identity and community meant that changing meaning and perception was not an easy task for the CBDC.

One strategy was to organize concerts, powerboat races and firework displays funded by the CBDC. Large numbers of visitors have attended these, with 2.1 million visits in 1998 to Cardiff's millennium waterfront (almost all of them in cars, which has generated a huge demand for car parking spaces). Clearly, encouraging such visitors builds legitimacy for the CBDC in the Cardiff area, though not particularly among Butetown residents. A second strategy has been giving new names to existing places. 'Cardiff Bay' is not a term which was ever used prior to the redevelopment. Today, however, buses indicate that 'Cardiff Bay' is their destination, and the local railway station has changed from 'Bute Road' to 'Cardiff Bay'. Clearly, power is implicated in devising and imposing new names for existing locations and structures. 'Cardiff Bay' connects with the familiar 'Tiger Bay', but carries a very different set of associations. Huw Thomas and Rob Imrie (1993) have pointed out that the various new developments have been given maritime-themed names ('Admiral's Landing' and 'Windsor Quay') which are rather lacking in historical basis: Cardiff docks were used by coal tramps, and never had any 'Admiral's Landing' nor was there ever a 'Windsor Quay'. 'Atlantic Wharf' (see Figure 10) is the new name for the more humble Bute East Dock – a part of the effort to associate Cardiff with the global stage, using a maritime theme.

FIGURE 12 *Cover of Cardiff Bay for Leisure brochure*

We know that photographs don't carry any inherent truth. Indeed, one of the two photographs in Figures 12 and 13 almost claims to be a photomontage, or computer-generated. But nonetheless they carry meanings.

What meanings do you see as carried by the various components of Figures 12 and 13? How might the 'vibrant' photograph make a Butetown resident feel marginalized?

FIGURE 13   Magazine advertisement for Cardiff Bay, May 1992

Establishing new meanings is not an easy task. Although the CBDC had a powerful publicity machine, a substantial budget, and the support of local media and politicians, its redevelopment vision was not unchallenged: there were limits to the power of its discourse, of its capacity to shape debates. Indeed for the CBDC to achieve its ends, there was a need – as ever in politics – to communicate a message, to develop legitimacy for the proposals, to carry people. Social strategies assisted the legitimation of its authority. The CBDC distributed something over £13 million to community projects between 1987 and 1998, including grants to community arts projects and educational organizations. Although it is an authority, it has to establish its authority – a distinction John Allen used in Book 3, Chapter 1.

An irony of these strategies of persuasion was that as well as threatening the local community, the CBDC has enabled new forms of struggle. The CBDC had to communicate its vision, but doing this opened up new channels for the Bay community to express its aspirations, and around which to focus its energy and sense of identity.

ACTIVITY 22

You should now read the following account (Reading 10) of *Making Waves*, a free newspaper which circulated in Butetown in the 1990s.

Before doing so you should note that the CBDC and the Cardiff Bay development, although focused on the waterfront in Butetown, covered an area much larger than Butetown, including substantial chunks of neighbouring wards in Penarth (across the River Taff) as well as Grangetown, Splott and Tremorfa in Cardiff. A key issue in the reading which follows is that residents of Butetown managed to appropriate this CBDC initiative, so that *Making Waves* focused very much on Butetown.

Issue No 112   **January 2000**

The Dawn Of A New Era

Photo by John Sinclair

CARDIFF's docklands have been regenerated, new hotels and buildings have been erected, Techniquest has been housed in a wonderful new setting, restaurants, bars and new retail outlets proliferate. The old landmarks have all but gone and new works of art have sprouted all over the place, some more accessible and appealing than others.

The Barrage controversy continues to rage, and will probably do so for some time to come. New housing developments with suitably nautical names such as Adventurers Quay, have attracted interest from wealthy home buyers and Bute Avenue is presently under construction, providing a grand link from the city centre to the Bay.

In a few weeks' time Cardiff Bay Development Corporation will be no more than a memory. Their remit was to transform a derelict area into a vibrant, thriving and prosperous attraction for both commercial interest and the tourist trade. Some would say that they have succeeded admirably. Old diehards will no doubt feel that their area has been irredeemably altered and not for the better. The true answer probably lies somewhere in the middle. It cannot be gainsaid that the transformation is dramatic, that tourists do come in their thousands and new roads and restaurants can be no bad thing.

There is a lingering regret, however, that the people who were here before the developers came, and who will still be here when the developers have gone, were not consulted at the outset, that more consideration was not given to them and more not done for them.

History will decide who is right.

INSIDE: Recipe p2, Bay Bouquet p3, Justice for ALL p4-5, Entertainment, Competition p6-7, CAB Advice Column p10, Days gone by p11

FIGURE 14 Front cover of *Making Waves,* issue number 112, January 2000

As you read the extract from Thomas *et al.*, note:

- the structures you can identify in the account,

- the agency which is being exercised, and

- any links which you can identify between structure and agency.

Huw Thomas *et al.*: 'Locality, urban governance and contested meanings of place'

Making Waves: origins and organisation

Making Waves, a free newspaper, was founded in 1990 as a joint initiative of Fullemploy (a national charity) and a group of agencies – including CBDC – active in the Docks, as a training and employment newsletter with a particular concern for equal opportunity issues. Its funding and management structure have continued to reflect this original remit. It is now one of a number of separately funded projects of Newemploy Wales (the reincarnation in Wales of the now deceased Fullemploy), in whose premises it is housed. Newemploy Wales's General Manager is the line manager of the editor of *Making Waves*, and she (a black English woman) is one of two people who read the newspaper *before* publication and, in effect, vet its content. As well as this support in kind from Newemploy, *Making Waves* receives financial assistance from: CBDC (largest source), the local TEC (Training & Enterprise Council), the City Council and the Employment Service. It also generates its own income, largely through selling advertising space; in 1994 it is to generate 33 per cent of total income, rising to 45 per cent in 1995 from this source.

Making Waves has two full-time staff, who do most things, including writing copy, taking photographs, and delivering door to door when necessary. As well as the line management structure referred to previously, the newspaper has a Review Board consisting of representatives of its funders, one 'community representative', one 'union member' and the general manager of Newemploy Wales. This meets every two months to discuss recent issues, and comment on general policy. The Board used to meet every month; and its less frequent meeting at present might be regarded as increasing the influence of the General Manager and the chair of the Review Board, CBDC's Community Development Office, who jointly vet each issue prior to publication, and have required changes on occasion.

This brief description of *Making Waves* shows that it is an illustration of the trends in local governance [...] inasmuch as CBDC's involvement – based on funding – is at 'arm's length'. It is this quasi-autonomous state of *Making Waves* which differentiates it from increasingly common local authority newsletters, and which opens up the possibility, at least, of its providing a platform and focus for independent, even oppositional, voices, for its fulfilling a function in creating part of Herbst's 'alternative public space'.

Content, focus and constructions of community

An example of the kind of opportunity which the paper's existence can create is the quarterly supplement *Bay Originals*, an initiative of the editor (herself a poet). *Bay Originals* carries writings by residents of the Bay or people who wish to write about the Bay. Its separate funding (Arts Council) from the paper, undoubtedly takes *Making Waves* in a direction not envisaged by the funding agencies. *Bay Originals* is very popular, and attracts and publishes (generally) nostalgic pieces (poetry, fiction and reminiscences) about the Bay as it was in its 'heyday'. In practice, these contributions tend not to be about the Cardiff Bay areas as presently defined, but about the Butetown area – part of which was also known as 'the Bay' (or 'Tiger Bay'). This geographical narrowing is important, because there are well documented cases of the ways in which nostalgia can be used to defuse contemporary social conflict and even promote regressive constructions of locality (see for example Brownill 1994 on the hijacking of the term 'docker' by London Docklands Development Corporation). The history of Butetown, however, is so bound up with racism, segregation and stigmatisation that the very act of recollecting and discussing the past, particularly if done systematically [...] is subversive of the 'colour-blind' policies and programmes of CBDC. Even the rose-tinted elements of residents' recollections often revolve around 'race' – they emphasise the way in which 'colour and creed' counted for nothing in Butetown. So a project conceived as a newsletter to inform people of training and employment opportunities has acquired a significant role as a forum, (for a time) the *only* forum of its kind – where Butetown's residents can explore and expand upon their own versions of their community's history. What these are will be discussed later.

The orientation towards Butetown (not part of the paper's brief) is evident in every aspect of the paper's coverage, as a simple count of the spatial focus of various kinds of content in the paper reveals. For example, in samples of 6 issues from 1990, 1992 and 1994 (18 issues in all), 50 per cent of letters published come from or mention Butetown; Butetown is mentioned in over two-thirds of front page news items in 1990 and 1992 (and though only in just under one-third of those in 1994, it still has more mentions than any other single area, except 'the Bay', which has one more mention). In all three years 50 per cent of 'other news' items refer to Butetown. If anything, these statistics underplay the feel of the paper as a Butetown project. Some big Butetown stories – for example, the story of the annual Carnival – can feature for a number of successive issues, allowing progress, problems, acknowledgements of assistance, etc to be discussed and noted in some detail. It is therefore evident why the local county councillor in interview might quite naturally refer to *Making Waves* as Butetown's 'community newspaper'. How this state of affairs has arisen is not entirely clear. The original remit to give some attention to equal opportunities issues would perhaps be interpreted by many in Cardiff (including editorial staff) as an implicit concern with Butetown in particular, which has a 46 per cent ethnic minority population but – more importantly – has been stigmatised for a century as a dangerous, explosive, multi-racial mix. But there has also been a response to the paper from people in Butetown which has propelled it, somewhat uncertainly at times, along a particular trajectory. As one of the editorial staff put it, the paper has 'street cred'.

Yet it is equally reasonable to hold that it *is not* a community newspaper, inasmuch as it remains dependent on the largesse of patrons from outside the area. The editor has been discouraged from campaigning (though the editorial staff claim that criticisms of CBDC or other agencies or individuals in letters are not censored). The front page headlines are relentlessly up-beat, reflecting a message which CBDC and other agencies involved in economic development wish to convey: that there *is* a future for local residents (though local unemployment rates show no sign of falling). The focus on individual examples of 'success' ignores the question of whether the CBDC has effected changes in the labour market which systematically open up new opportunities for Butetown's residents – in particular, has it challenged the processes which ensure that 'in Cardiff, people from minorities ... are still broadly confined, after all these years, to unskilled, semi-skilled or basic clerical jobs in manufacturing, food processing, transport and health services' (CRE (Commission for Racial Equality) 1991, 44). Certain classes of issue, which might be the staple fare of community newspapers elsewhere do not feature – notably, housing issues. The omissions, the tone, the style, combine to present a particular construction of Butetown in the 1990s: it is of an historically disadvantaged and marginalised community being integrated into the mainstream of modern economic life (not necessarily without struggle). True to its original remit, the paper is scrupulous in using photographs (especially), and also text, to convey the message that these opportunities will not be subject to racism or sexism. The implication is that Cardiff Bay's urban regeneration *does* hold out hope for Butetown; that racial discrimination was part of a less modern, less meritocratic social order, a crude system of social control, which will be swept away if CBDC is successful. The racialised identification of the community with the territory of the Bay will also be unnecessary and its loss not especially to be regretted. This construction seems to touch on powerful local sentiments in two respects. First, one strand in the upbeat portrayal of the area highlights self-help (for example, 'Homework Clubs', where local teachers help local children; or new businesses started by local people); and this, it is plausible to surmise, strikes a chord in an area whose population is long used to developing strategies for survival in a generally hostile world. Secondly, there are mixed emotions about the kind of community Butetown is taken to have been in the past – warm and tolerant it may have been, but it was also poor and stigmatised, and some residents (such as the African county councillor [...]) recognise racism, struggle against it, but have no particular desire to organise around racial or ethnic identities. One source of influence this (African) county councillor has in the community, is being chair of a residents association, a *territorial* base, rather than a 'racial' base. They might welcome the idea that racial/ethnic identities may be less significant in a prosperous dockland community. For these reasons, the appropriate vocabulary and imagery for expressing residents' views about CBDC's project is *not* one which draws up clear battle-lines around being for or against. The concerns of residents as expressed at community meetings we have attended, relate to what the changes will mean for their way of life, their community, their area.

These concerns find no place in the 'official line' of *Making Waves*, but an alternative (not necessarily wholly antagonistic) discussion of identity and territoriality is also taking place, with the newspaper providing what Herbst calls an appropriate 'discourse environment'. The newspaper editor remarked that the term 'Tiger Bay' was more in evidence of late than she could ever remember. Not only is this so in relation to *Making Waves*; the themes of recent annual carnivals, organised by people in their twenties and thirties, have focused on Tiger Bay, and emphasised its multi-racial/multi-cultural history and present character. There is an openness, an assertiveness in acknowledging Butetown's history (which is shot through with racism and its consequences) which is new. A local 'history workshop' project, which collects photographs, etc, inevitably has a critical edge which similar popular activities do not always have. There is a great deal of sentimentality too, as the *Bay Originals* supplement can testify, but sentimentality, within bounds, is sometimes an appropriate reaction to social disruption; in any event, in the Cardiff of the 1990s, the photographs of multi-racial schoolrooms, families and parties, even if 'historic', still mark out Butetown as distinctive. Whereas the upbeat 'Butetown is modernising' message is sustained by editorial copy, the references to the history of Butetown, its values, its cultural mix, etc, are sustained by voluntary contributions (letters, poems, photographs). These contributions make no overt claims, sustain no sophisticated argument about identity and territory, but in the context of CBDC's welter of publicity and promotional hype about the new Cardiff Bay (including the changing of names of bus routes, a railway station and road signs) then the exchange of correspondence about the origins of the name 'Tiger Bay', the reminiscences, the arguments over prospects of employment, constitute significant evidence of an alternative set of views and concerns being expressed (albeit, at times, obliquely). Such activity does constitute a claim to territory: it is a reminder that whatever promises are made about the future, the history of the area justifies priority in the distribution of benefits being given to current residents.

These illustrations of alternative views being expressed in *Making Waves* return us to the question of what influence they may have over CBDC. This is a complex question to which ultimately no definitive answer may be possible on the available evidence. However, Herbst's conceptual framework does point us towards an important prior question, namely *how* might influence be wielded by the alternative public sphere of which *Making Waves* seems a part. Her notion of 'backchannels', of networks of sympathetic individuals forming a link between the 'mainstream' and 'parallel' public spheres directs us to the significance, in Cardiff Bay, of people such as the editor of *Making Waves*. On the one hand she meets CBDC officers regularly to discuss the paper; on the other, she has been instrumental in helping to create space in the newspaper where Butetown residents can express themselves on the question of identity and territory.

The editor is not the only person who is part of a 'backchannel'; the local county councillor referred to earlier, reads *Making Waves* and understands its value as a guide to what some in the community are thinking. In his official capacity as a councillor and a chair of a local residents' group he also meets officers of CBDC, including the Chief Executive. Similarly, he provides a link between the alternative public sphere and political discussion in the local Labour Party and the county council. It is plausible to suggest, therefore, that whatever influence *Making Waves* may have in the 'mainstream' of Cardiff's political life will be exercised through the development of backchannels, such as those previously illustrated. An important empirical question relating to local governance which then arises [...] is whether the creation of such backchannels is *easier* in the fragmented local governance system, of which UDCs (Urban Development Corporation) are a part, than in the traditional system where local authorities dominated.

References

Brownill, S. (1994) 'Selling the inner city: regeneration and place marketing in London's Docklands', in Gold, J. and Ward, S.V. (eds) *Place Promotion* (John Wiley, Chichester).

Commission for Racial Equality (1991) *Employers in Cardiff* (CRE, London).

Herbst, S. (1994) *Politics at the Margin* (Cambridge University Press, Cambridge).

Source: Thomas *et al.*, 1996, pp.192–6

C O M M E N T

Among the structures we noted were the CBDC and the other bodies which funded *Making Waves*.

Regarding agency, Thomas *et al.* argue that *Making Waves*, funded as it was 'at arm's length', provided a platform for oppositional or independent voices.

At a broad level, structure and agency are linked inasmuch as the dominant structure, the CBDC, by supporting *Making Waves*, provoked organization and expression – 'backchannels' is the expression Thomas *et al.* use.

A key specific link between structure and agency which Thomas *et al.* make is that individuals' experience and identities are so bound up with racism and segregation in Butetown that recollecting history constitutes a challenge to powerful institutions.

A part of Butetown's distinct and isolated history has been its self-organization.

> What they had in common were experiences of seafaring and of discrimination [...] Encouraged by leaders of varying origins, despite the fear instilled by the Chief Constable, the state and the employers, and the problems caused by intermittent absences, they also united into more comprehensive organisations to assert their rights and struggle against discriminatory practice by the employers, the unions, the city and the state [...]
>
> But, however mighty the racist power of all those allied against them, the people of The Bay resisted and survived with dignity.
>
> (Sherwood, 1991, pp.67–8)

So the nature of the community and its history equipped the people of Butetown for dealing with the CBDC. They too had a wide repertoire of strategies. Consider the structures and agency involved in the following short account of the Butetown Carnival Committee.

This informal (and changing) group of local people organised an annual carnival, essentially as a local entertainment, though [...] carnival is also an expression of popular control and enjoyment of particular spaces. CBDC became interested in grant-aiding the event, but only if it became a significant visitor attraction. Committee members were encouraged to look to London, Bristol and elsewhere as examples of the potential of the event. Very modest financial support was accompanied by attempts to force the organisation to become considerably more formal and entrepreneurial; faced by local recalcitrance, CBDC hired a multicultural arts project from outside the area to run workshops for local children (with expertise imported from Latin America) on aspects of carnival (costume making and so on), a move which is most plausibly interpreted as an attempt to change the meaning of the carnival and of its claim to space [...] After a few years, the development corporation ran out of patience, and the carnival committee felt it preferable to retain control, albeit with a smaller budget: a modest attempt by CBDC to reinterpret some of Butetown's spaces had failed.

(Thomas, 1999, p.15)

4.5 Conclusion and summary

In this account of the redevelopment of Cardiff Bay we have identified a range of structures which are involved in a process of urban development. We have seen that power is not monolithic, but contested, by both institutions and individuals or groups. The form and scope of such a contest is very much set by the particularities of the Cardiff situation; its history, its economy, its culture, and its politics. So to make sense of the redevelopment we have to take account of global structures and forces, UK national, Welsh national, and Cardiff local forces. We have seen that an account of these agencies, institutions and structures, however, is only a part of the story. Their powers, although considerable, depend in large part for their success on constructing new meanings for Butetown – with its new name, Cardiff Bay. But meanings are historically rooted, and bound up with identities and communities; they are not easily changed. Thus the agency involved in this story is not simply a question of resistance, an account like David and Goliath. It is a story of structured power, but it shows that structures and power are complex. To exercise its power, the CBDC has to engage in contests about the meanings of Cardiff Bay. And in doing so it opens up channels for the expression of opposition and the development or reinforcement of local identities. The outcome of this struggle is in some senses remarkable. True, the barrage is built and the bistros and wine bars are open on the waterfront. But the CBDC has been abolished, and the community seems in some ways stronger than it was before the start. Maybe there was some grain of truth in the CBDC appeal to outside investors, that this was 'Europe's most exciting waterfront development'.

The extent to which this is the case, of course, depends – amongst other factors – on how much local residents recognize the authority of the bodies which govern them. Whilst these bodies, these authorities, these structures, seek to achieve domination by constraint and removing choice, the extent to which residents of Cardiff Bay internalize this constraint is not fixed or certain. Clearly, it is shaped by structured inequalities, and by material resources. But at some point – and this draws on Foucault's model of power – we are free to govern ourselves. The ideology of redevelopment constrains or shapes the discourse, but does not control it. In this way we can see the power of agency and the possibilities for contestation.

As with Section 3.5, we suggest you give yourself some time now to summarize your own notes on structure and agency and link the account in Block 6 to earlier blocks in the course. Our notes, below, are for comparison only, you need to make your own!

---

1   Structure is a term used generically to describe any patterning or system that shapes human action. In DD100 we have looked at biological structures (including genetic structures of the body and the external environment); cultural structures (languages, discourses, stereotypes); economic structures (markets, firms); political structures (states, bureaucracies, quangos); and material structures (urban layouts, telecommunication infrastructures).

2   Structures come in different forms. In DD100 we have distinguished between relatively fixed, enduring institutions, public and private, formal and informal; and broader patterns of social stratification such as class, occupation, gender, and ethnicity or 'race'.

3   In DD100 we have also distinguished between the different spatial levels at which structures exist and exert their effects: global, regional, national, local.

4   Shifting between these different spatial levels of analysis demonstrates that many institutions can be thought of as both structures and agencies depending on what we are looking at. Cardiff has a structured distribution of work, wealth and power which shapes its inhabitants' agency, but Cardiff itself is an agent in the global marketplace for investment.

5   Structures, of whatever kind, shape agency in a number of ways. We can distinguish between conscious and unconscious constraint. We can distinguish between different mechanisms of constraint – stereotypes, roles, discourses, direct coercion, and authority.

    Structures not only constrain and limit agency but provide the resources necessary for agency, such as power, wealth, and meanings. Structures create opportunities for agency as well, though of course these are invariably distributed in very unequal ways.

6   The ways in which structures both create and distribute power depend on the types of agency we are looking at, and the theory of power we are

using. Agents can use power directly, but power works on and through agents.

7 Agency can be both individual and collective. Agency can be both direct and intended, and indirect and unintended in its consequences. Agents constantly interact with one another, these interactions can be competitive, conflictual or co-operative.

8 One of the key unintended consequences of agency is the reproduction of structures, be they economic, cultural, etc. So, for example, language speakers as agents draw on the structures of vocabulary and grammar to create sentences and speech, but in doing so they also reaffirm and entrench those rules and structures. However, language speakers are also capable of innovation (new words, turns of phrase) and deviation (speaking ungrammatically). If repeated sufficiently these kinds of innovation and deviation change the structures of language.

Innovation, deviation and challenges by human agents lie at the core of processes of structural change.

5 KNOWLEDGE, KNOWING AND THE CITY

5.1 The argument: cities, knowledge and communication

As we argued in Sections 2.4 and 2.5 of this *End of Course Review*, the city in the UK is being transformed both by the increasing importance of information and communication technologies and by the increasing importance of knowledge workers and companies in the wider economy. Both of these shifts are global in their extent and in their impact. It is one thing to argue that there is a connection between these shifts and the character of UK cities. However, it is quite another to establish precisely what that connection is and what the most likely set of changes associated with it will be. Broadly speaking, accounts of this interrelationship fall into two camps: optimists and pessimists. To get a flavour of these arguments we are going to begin this section with two short extracts which outline these two scenarios. Francis Cairncross, whose work you will have met in Book 5, Chapter 4, is an optimist. Robert Reich, an American economist, is a pessimist. His work uses the notion of symbolic analysts – a term that tries to capture the increasingly significant and powerful groups of knowledge workers who create, manipulate, and interpret information and knowledge in all sectors of the economy. His work is focused on the experience of the USA, and the bias this induces should be borne in mind. However, there are important connections to the UK experience.

ACTIVITY 23

Read and make short notes on the core arguments of the following readings.

Francis Cairncross: 'The death of distance'

[...] the main impact of the death of distance will be to make communication and access to information in all its forms more convenient. On balance, that will surely be good for societies everywhere, although the nature of the effect will depend on why people communicate and what knowledge they choose to acquire and how they use it. Like the automobile, telecommunications technology will be a tool that can be used for bad purposes as well as good, but it should, overall, make people's lives easier and richer. More communication is nearly always better than less.

In broad terms, the societies of the rich world may be altered in four main ways. The role of the home will change. The home will reacquire functions that it has lost over the past century. It will become not just a workshop, but a place where people receive more of their education, training, and health care. New kinds of community will develop, bonded electronically across distance, sharing work, domestic interests, and cultural backgrounds. Both the use of the English language and the strength of local cultures will be enhanced. English will be the standard global tongue, but many regional languages will revive, as well. And, finally, the young, and especially the intelligent and well-educated young, will be the winners in the new electronic world, and young countries will gain an advantage over older ones. [...]

Amid the speculations is one certainty: the falling price of communications will affect where people work and live. The old demarcation between work and home will evaporate. In its place will be a shift in the location of work, a new role for cities, a new role for the home, and reshaped communities. Of these, the third may be the most profound. [...]

In the past century, people have tended to live farther and farther from their place of employment. Instead of living on the farm or over the shop, people have moved from city centers to suburbs and from suburbs to commuter towns. In some cities, almost all the decline in working hours in this century has been gobbled up in increased commuting time.

One of the main reasons for this trend has been the concentration of employment in large units. Through the first half of the century, the size of the factory, and then of the office, tended to grow. With factories in most rich countries, this trend had begun to reverse by the 1970s, mainly as a result of the rise in productivity.

Now, the nature of working life is starting to change again. A primary shift in the location of work will affect people in three main categories: routine teleworking jobs, vehicle-based jobs, and jobs involving top-level personal contact.

Initially, teleworking jobs will be concentrated in large units. A bank no longer needs as many small branches once people can do more of their banking by telephone and by other electronic means; a travel agent no longer needs as many people in local offices. Such activities can be handled by a single call center, which does not need to be located in a particular city. The activity becomes centralized, but the place of work can be decentralized.

Some teleworkers will work from home. Various experiments have found a number of benefits in working from home. Foremost is more job satisfaction and lower stress. A trial by Northern Telecom in 1994 found a 30 percent increase in productivity when five hundred employees worked from home at least three days per week. Another benefit is increased flexibility in working hours. A one-year experiment conducted in the far north of Scotland by Britain's BT, the country's primary telephone company, found that home-based directory-assistance operators, connected to a supervisor and the customer by a telephone line and a computer link, were more reliable. Environmental benefits also accrue from home-based workers. Results from a trial sponsored by AT&T in Phoenix, Arizona, in the early 1990s, suggested that if 1 percent of all workers in private and public organizations of one hundred employees or more telecommuted one day each week, fuel consumption would be cut by almost 500,000 gallons per year.

Electronic home-working has, of course, some significant drawbacks, as well. Connection to a high-capacity fiber-optic network constitutes an expensive investment. If employers carry the cost, they will do so initially only for the workers with the most valuable and irreplaceable output. Maintenance costs will also be high. When connections or equipment break down, repairs may be easier in a central office than for workers scattered around the country. As long as their equipment is out of action, so, too, are the teleworkers. [...]

Mobile communications will allow the growth of a whole category of workers – many of them engaged in various kinds of maintenance work or in delivery (of people as well as goods) – whose days will be structured by controllers using a mixture of satellite positioning equipment to track their teams, computers to calculate the most efficient routes, and mobile telephones with messaging systems to maintain contact between dispatchers and workers.

Safeway, for example, Britain's third-largest supermarket chain [...] uses satellite tracking to follow the movements of its six hundred trucks, reducing delays and streamlining delivery routes. An increasing number of workers will thus, as it were, telework from a vehicle rather than from home.

Many senior employees will find themselves doing their work almost anywhere but in the office. The number of 'portfolio' workers – non-executive directors, consultants, and one-person agencies who combine several senior-level freelance jobs under contracts with different companies – will grow. Such people will not have an extensive corporate structure behind them. They will keep their own complicated diaries, sift their own mail (as, electronically, Bill Gates of Microsoft is said to do), and handle their own intricate travel arrangements. They will work partly out of their homes and partly out of cabs or airport departure lounges.

Airports and airplanes will be, increasingly, temporary offices for senior people, who, ironically, will spend more time on the road as a result of better communications, even as the same communications decrease the time their staffs spend commuting. To hold together businesses with global scope, which will often have production and distribution spread among several countries requires not only an efficient electronic network but an enormous amount of travel by managers and suppliers. For these people, living near a good airport may be even more important than living near the head office. They will need and want portable offices: a multipurpose mobile telephone that will receive messages, send faxes, contact the office database, and tap into the Internet. For them, the most advanced communications will be godsends, as along as the equipment and services deliver what they promise and work reliably.

These workers may also operate from restaurants, at conferences, in golf clubs. All these venues provide a much more appropriate backdrop than the office for the face-to-face contacts that are central to many service industries. A senior partner in an advertising agency cannot deal with clients entirely by telephone any more than can a high-powered lawyer or a Hollywood agent. These personal contacts require a structured informality, a blend of the personal and the professional. The telephone and electronic mail may reinforce basic contacts, but they cannot substitute for face-to-face encounters.

What of the office? It will become the place for the social aspects of work, such as networking, lunch, and catching up on office gossip. The familiar roles of home and office will thus be inverted. The provision of a good office canteen, sports facilities, and plenty of meeting rooms will become more important; the individual office, with a large desk and lots of storage space, less so. The office will become a 'club', a transformation spotted by Charles Handy, a British management guru. The office-as-club will foster a sense of fellowship (or corporate culture) among employees, stimulating conversation and belonging; it will be the main site at which companies stimulate workers and mold them into teams; and it will provide a location for training, communicating, and brainstorming.

In the future, then, much more work will be done outside offices. Some will take place in transit, some in the home. That will have long-term consequences for city centers, where in the twentieth century work has increasingly been located.

In half a century's time, it may well seem extraordinary that millions of people once trooped from one building (their home) to another (their office) each morning, only to reverse the procedure each evening. Commuting requires a transport network built to cope with these two peak daily migrations. Roads must accommodate the weight of rush-hour traffic, and commuter railways and buses must carry the mass of peak-load passengers. Commuting wastes time and building capacity. One building – the home – often stands empty all day; another – the office, often in the most expensive part of town – usually stands empty all night. All this may strike our grandchildren as bizarre.

The dispersion of work will alter the nature of cities and towns, reaffirming their importance as places where people live and as centers for entertainment and culture. More people will return to living in city centers. Cities with attractive architecture and plenty of shops and cafes providing lively street life will delight those who relish the bustle and the anonymity of living in a crowd. Cities will become even more attractive as they become safer, thanks to wider use of electronic surveillance. Cities will also thrive as centers of entertainment and culture: places to which people travel for a stay in a hotel, a museum or gallery visit, a restaurant meal, or to hear a concert or band. Many kinds of work will require entertainment: managers will increasingly want to take valued customers to a theater, a restaurant, a club. So some of these delights will be paid for, directly or indirectly, by companies.

Suburbs and rural towns will benefit from the telecommunications revolution in other ways. Many people may once again 'live over the shop' and work in their communities, rather than commuting. The benefits will include more revenue for local stores and other services, as workers stay close to their hometowns during the weekday; more opportunities for delivery services, since ordering over the Internet or telephone becomes easier if someone is at home when the product reaches the doorstep; and less local crime, because homes will be occupied and streets will be busy during the day, making them safer for everyone.

All these changes will have a darker side. The fragmentation of the large employer has made many workers feel less secure. More and more people, employed on short-term contracts or as freelancers, will be only as good as their last job and under constant pressure to find the next assignment before the current one finishes. The blending of leisure and work may well mean, in practice, that work increasingly intrudes into leisure: it makes the more forceful demands. Besides, working at home, however sophisticated the electronic links, lacks the companionship of working alongside other human beings. And, of course, not every downtown office complex, if deprived of office tenants, will be quickly transformed into a glittering entertainment center. But on balance, the direction of change may be to restore communities, to improve the quality of cities, and to give people more control over their working lives.

Source: Cairncross, 1997, pp.233–9

READING 12

Robert Reich: 'The new community'

The hypothesis that some degree of rational calculation, rather than simple delusion, underlies the disengagement of **symbolic analysts** from the broader public is evinced by how the symbolic analyst has chosen to live. In allocating personal income, the symbolic analyst has shown no lack of willingness to engage in collective investment. But increasingly, the public goods that result are shared only with other symbolic analysts. Symbolic analysts take on the responsibilities of citizenship, but the communities they create are composed only of citizens with incomes close to their own. In this way, symbolic analysts are quietly seceding from the large and diverse publics [...] into homogeneous enclaves, within which their earnings need not be redistributed to people less fortunate than themselves.

Symbolic analysts Reich's term for the class of people whose occupations and income are derived from the creation and manipulation of data and symbols of all kinds – architects, computer programmers, media workers, etc.

The pattern is familiar. With each sought-after reduction in their taxes, symbolic analysts in effect withdraw their dollars from the support of public spaces shared by all and dedicate the savings to private spaces they share with other symbolic analysts. As public parks and playgrounds deteriorate, there is a proliferation of private health clubs, golf clubs, tennis clubs, skating clubs, and every other type of recreational association in which costs are divided up among members. So also with condominiums, cooperatives, and the omnipresent 'residential communities' which dun their members in order to undertake efforts that financially strapped local governments can no longer afford to do well – maintaining private roadways, mending sidewalks, pruning trees, repairing streetlights, cleaning swimming pools and paying for a lifeguard, and – notably – hiring security guards to protect life and property. By 1990, private security

In-person servers
A class of occupations and services which require the physical presence of the worker – cleaning, nursing, etc.

guards comprised fully 2.6 percent of the nation's work force, double the percentage in 1970, and outnumbering public police officers in the United States. Taking note of this striking growth, the Bureau of Labor Statistics has accorded the occupation the honor of a separate job category all its own. With revenues of the ten largest guard companies rising 62 percent in the 1980s, in real terms, private security was one of the fastest-growing industries in the United States (even faster than the legal profession).[1]

The same pattern of secession has been apparent on a grander scale in America's major cities. By the 1990s, most urban centers had splintered, in effect, into two separate cities – one composed of symbolic analysts whose conceptual services were linked to the world economy; the other, of **in-person servers** (custodial, security, taxi, clerical, parking, retail sales, restaurant) whose jobs were dependent on the symbolic analysts.[2] Few routine producers remained within America's cities. Between 1953 and 1984, for example, New York City lost about 600,000 routine factory jobs; during the same interval, it added about 700,000 symbolic-analytic and in-person service jobs.[3] In Pittsburgh, routine production jobs dropped from almost half the city's employment in 1953 to less than 20 percent by the mid-1980s; the other two categories made up the difference, as the city amassed America's third-largest concentration of corporate headquarters.[4]

The separation of symbolic analysts from in-person servers within cities has been reinforced in several ways. By the 1990s, most large cities possessed two school systems – a private one for the children of symbolic analysts and a public one for the children of in-person servers, the few remaining routine producers, and the unemployed.[5] Symbolic analysts are known to spend considerable time and energy ensuring that their children gain entrance to good private schools, and then small fortunes keeping them there – dollars that under a more progressive tax code could have financed better public education. The separation also has been maintained by residential patterns. Symbolic analysts live in areas of the city that, if not beautiful, are at least aesthetically tolerable and reasonably safe; precincts not meeting these minimum standards of charm and security have been left to those less fortunate.

Here again, symbolic analysts have pooled their resources – to the exclusive benefit of themselves. Public funds have been applied in earnest to downtown 'revitalization' projects, entailing the construction of clusters of postmodern office buildings (replete with fiber-optic cables, private branch exchanges, satellite dishes, and other state-of-the-art transmission and receiving equipment), multilevel parking garages, hotels with glass-enclosed atriums rising twenty stories or higher, upscale shopping plazas and gallerias, theaters, convention centers, and luxury condominiums. Ideally, the projects are entirely self-contained, with air-conditioned walk-ways linking residential, business, and recreation functions. The fortunate symbolic analyst is thankfully able to shop, work, and attend the theater without risking direct contact with the outside world – in particular, the other city.[6] [...]

When not living in urban enclaves, symbolic analysts have congregated in residential suburbs and, increasingly, in what are termed 'exurbs' in the surrounding countryside. The most desirable of such locations border symbolic-analytic zones of universities, research parks, or corporate headquarters, in pleasant environs such as Princeton, New Jersey; northern Westchester and Putnam counties, New York; Palo Alto, California; Austin, Texas; Bethesda, Maryland; and Raleigh-Durham, North Carolina. American engineers and strategists employed by American-owned automobile companies, for example, do not live in Flint or Saginaw, Michigan, where the companies' routine workers reside; they cluster in their own towns of Troy, Warren, and Auburn Hills. The vast majority of the financial specialists, lawyers, and executives working for the insurance companies of Hartford would never consider living there; after all, Hartford is one of the poorest cities in the nation. Instead, they flock to Windsor, Middlebury, and other nearby Connecticut townships, which are, unsurprisingly, among the wealthiest in the nation.

Suburban and exurban townships like these offer another convenient means of secession into communities of comparable income. Property taxes in well-heeled communities serve much the same function as any other method of pooling resources among symbolic analysts while avoiding having to subsidize anyone else. In-person servers who provide symbolic analysts with house-cleaning, day-care, retail, restaurant, automotive, and related services tend to reside in poorer townships nearby, and thus do not share directly in local public amenities.

The federal government has cooperated in these efforts by shifting responsibility for many public services to state and local governments. Federal grants comprised almost 27 percent of state and local spending at their peak in 1978. Ten years later, the federal share had dwindled to 17 percent.[8] [...]

Cities and towns with wealthier inhabitants could, of course, bear these burdens relatively easily. Poorer jurisdictions, faced with the twin problems of lower incomes and a greater demand for social services, have had more difficulty. This is precisely the point: As Americans continue to segregate according to what they earn, the shift in financing public services from the federal government to the states, and from the states to cities and towns, has functioned as another means of relieving America's wealthier citizens of the burdens of America's less fortunate.

For most of the nation's history, poorer towns and regions steadily gained ground on wealthier areas, as American industry spread to Southern and Western states in search of cheaper labor. This trend ended sometime in the 1970s, as American industry moved on to Mexico, Southeast Asia, and other places around the world. Since then, most poorer towns and regions in the United States have grown relatively poorer; most wealthier towns and regions, relatively wealthier.

Footnotes

1. See 'The Growth of Private Security', in William C. Cunningham and Todd H. Taylor, *Private Security and Police in America* (Portland, Ore.: Chancellor Press, 1985). See also L. Uchitelle, 'Sharp Rise of Private Guard Jobs', *The New York Times*, October 14, 1989, p.A16. [...]

2. The trend has been confirmed on a number of studies. See, for example, Thierry Noyelle, *Beyond Industrial Dualism* (Boulder, Colo.: Westview Press, 1987); Saskia Sassen, *The Mobility of Labor and Capital* (Cambridge: Cambridge University Press, 1987); John Kasarda, 'Dual Cities: The New Structure of Urban Poverty', *New Perspectives Quarterly*, Winter 1987.

3. These data are from John Kasarda, 'Urban Industrial Transition and the Underclass', *Annals of the AAPSS*, January 1989.

4. B. Frieden and L. Sagalyn, *Downtown, Inc.: How America Rebuilds Cities* (Cambridge: MIT Press, 1989); see also J. Kasarda, 'Economic Restructuring and America's Urban Dilemma', in M. Dogan and J. Kasarda (eds), *Economic Restructuring and America's Urban Dilemma* (Beverly Hills, Calif.: Sage, 1988).

5. See, for example, Paul Ong *et al.*, 'Inequalities in Los Angeles', Graduate School of Architecture and Urban Planning, University of California at Los Angeles, June 1989.

6. See William Schmidt, 'Riding a Boom, Downtowns Are No Longer Down-trodden', *The New York Times*, October 11, 1987, p.A28. [...]

8. U.S. Advisory Commission on Intergovernmental Relations, *Significant Features of Fiscal Federalism* (1988 ed.), Vol.2, p.115. [...]

Source: Reich, 1991, pp.268–73

C O M M E N T

Our notes looked like this:

CAIRNCROSS: DEATH OF DISTANCE

1. Technology → social change, short term and long term; cf. the impact of cars and crime.

2. Many fear the communications revolution, i.e. privacy declines, inequalities in access to communications, global deluge of Hollywood culture.

3. But C. believes it's on balance good news.

4. Key transformations brought about:

   (a) role of home, relationship with work

   (b) character of communities

   (c) use of English as a global language, but revival of local cultures too

   (d) winners will be young, well-educated

5. 4(a) and (b) combine to influence the <u>fate of cities</u>

   In 20th C. home and work increasingly separate so increase in leisure time absorbed by commuting time in many cities.

In 20th C. concentration of employment in city centres and v. large units encourage this.

6   For 3 categories of workers this will cease as cost of communication declines:

   (a) Teleworkers → at home, benefits in productivity (Northern Telecom), flexibility (BT Scotland), environment (AT+T, Arizona) – but problems too

   (b) Vehicle using workers

      mobile telecoms → teleworking from vehicles, e.g. Safeway

   (c) High level workers

      need personal contact – travel for face-to-face meetings in very wide variety of contexts with mobile office

7   So office becomes the social club/place to network in and home becomes location of work.

8   So ... impacts on cities?

   -   old model of separation and community will appear wasteful and bizarre

   -   people → return to live in city centres

   -   CCTV will make them safer

   -   suburbs and rural towns will benefit too

   -   some decline of cities – but on balance good news.

REICH: THE NEW COMMUNITY

1   Symbolic analysts/knowledge workers (KW) – tend to live in communities with only other KW 'homogenous enclaves'. They are seceding geographically and financially from the rest of society.

2   KW seek low taxes – withdraw from public spaces and create own private spaces

   i.e. ↓ public parks → private leisure facilities

      ↓ public space → private ← security guards and valued commodities.

3   These divisions are entrenched by public expenditure on city centre redevelopment for KW (malls, etc. that exclude the poor) and creation of exurbs – connected to symbolic analyst zones of universities, research parks ...

4   This shift → vicious circle. Tax money is concentrated in richer areas that need it least and vice versa for poorer areas.

5   Evidence suggests that inequalities within and between US cities are consequently widening.

As you have probably noticed, there are plenty of connections between these arguments and material in both the *End of Course Review* and earlier blocks in DD100.

In particular we noted:

- Cairncross's emphasis on the role of technology in social change compares with the arguments for and against technological determinism in Book 4, Chapter 2, Section 5.

- Cairncross's model of the broad impact of the communications revolution was examined in Book 5, Chapter 4, Section 2.2 and links to both Bell's earlier account of post-industrialism and Leadbeater's account of the knowledge economy.

- Cairncross's optimism about the fate of city centres in an era of global telecommunications is closer to the model offered by Peter Hall in Section 2.5 of this *End of Course Review* – although Hall's argument is in some ways more developed. Ian Taylor (Reading 5) in Section 2.4 places much more emphasis on local growth coalitions, diversity between cities, and alternative regeneration strategies, as does Richard Rogers (Reading 2) in Section 2.2.

- Reich's account of divided cities and vicious downward circles of decay is closer to the post-Fordist arguments presented in Book 5, Chapter 4, Section 3 and Worpole's and Fyfe's accounts of change in UK cities in the 1990s (Readings 8 and 9).

- Reich draws on the accounts of changing labour markets in Book 3, Chapter 3, and the differential impact of crime in cities (*End of Course Review*, Section 3.4.2).

- Reich's polarization model can be compared usefully to Sassen (Reading 4) and Book 1, Chapter 3, Section 7.

We are going to examine all of these arguments in terms of their internal structure and their use of the *circuit of knowledge* in Section 5.3 below. Before we go on to do this, we have produced a diagram which picks out the main lines of argument about the future of the city.

We have two different views of the communications revolution and the knowledge economy. The first, optimistic view which focuses on the revival and reinvention of cities is represented by Francis Cairncross and the more pessimistic emphasis on the decline and fragmentation of cities by Robert Reich.

We have included some of the key sources in the *End of Course Review* and earlier parts of DD100 to produce Diagram I.

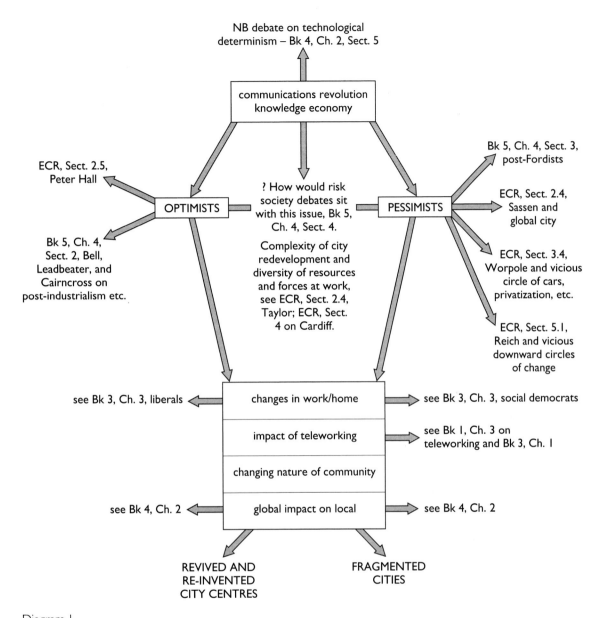

NB debate on technological
determinism – Bk 4, Ch. 2, Sect. 5

communications revolution
knowledge economy

ECR, Sect. 2.5,
Peter Hall

OPTIMISTS

? How would risk
society debates sit
with this issue, Bk 5,
Ch. 4, Sect. 4.

PESSIMISTS

Bk 5, Ch. 4, Sect. 3,
post-Fordists

ECR, Sect. 2.4,
Sassen and
global city

Bk 5, Ch. 4,
Sect. 2, Bell,
Leadbeater, and
Cairncross on
post-industrialism etc.

Complexity of city
redevelopment and
diversity of resources
and forces at work,
see ECR, Sect. 2.4,
Taylor; ECR, Sect.
4 on Cardiff.

ECR, Sect. 3.4,
Worpole and vicious
circle of cars,
privatization, etc.

ECR, Sect. 5.1,
Reich and vicious
downward circles
of change

see Bk 3, Ch. 3, liberals

changes in work/home

see Bk 3, Ch. 3, social democrats

impact of teleworking

see Bk 1, Ch. 3 on
teleworking and Bk 3, Ch. 1

changing nature of community

see Bk 4, Ch. 2

global impact on local

see Bk 4, Ch. 2

REVIVED AND
RE-INVENTED
CITY CENTRES

FRAGMENTED
CITIES

Diagram 1

5.2 Revisiting knowledge and knowing

In the *Mid Course Review*, we drew together the material on knowledge and knowing from the first four blocks of the course in a diagram which is reproduced in Figure 15.

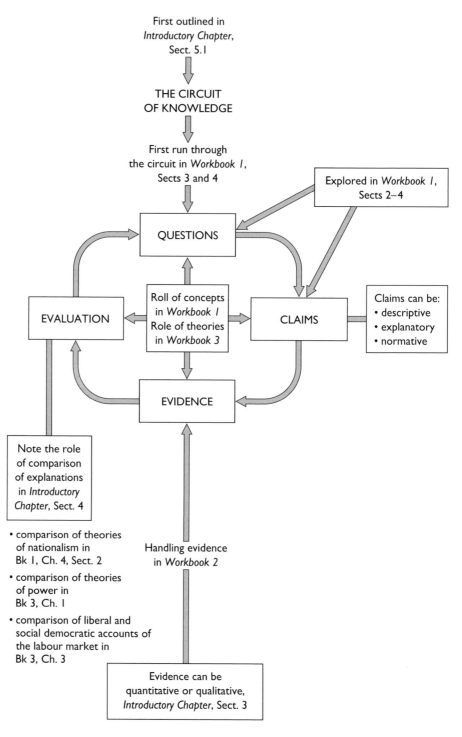

FIGURE 15

Knowledge and knowing: Introductory Block–Block 3

In Blocks 4 and 5 you will have covered a lot of additional ground, including the following.

- The *evaluation* of social science theories and arguments using the criteria of *coherence, empirical adequacy* and *comprehensiveness*. See especially:

  Workbook 4, Introduction, Sections 3.4, 4.2 and 5.1

  Book 5, Chapter 4, especially Section 5

  Workbook 5, Section 4.3.

- The relationship between *political ideologies, normative and political claims* and *social science arguments*. See especially:

  Workbook 4, Sections 2.4 and 5.1

  Book 5, Chapter 3

  Workbook 5, Sections 3.1 and 3.3.

- The social construction of knowledge in general and social science knowledge in particular with special reference to the role of language, power and institutions. See especially:

  Book 5, Introduction, Chapter 1, and Afterword

  Audio-cassette 9, Side B.

- Comparing social science knowledge with other forms of knowledge, especially the natural sciences, and the distinction in both natural and social sciences between verification and falsification. See especially:

  Book 5, Chapter 1

  Workbook 5, Section 1.2.

- Comparing how different traditions in the social sciences approach the whole question of *knowledge and knowing* in different ways. See especially:

  Book 5, Chapter 2 on comparison of positivism and interpretative social science

  Workbook 5, Section 2.3.

- Finally, since our last review of *knowledge and knowing* you will have revisited the place of evidence in the *circuit of knowledge* in a number of ways. See especially:

  Study Skills Supplement 2: Reading Evidence, comparing the strengths and weaknesses of quantitative evidence

  Book 4, Chapters 2 and 3, and *Workbook 4*, Section 2.3 on use and presentation of quantitative evidence

  Study Skills Supplement 3: Reading Maps on reading and using a very particular type of evidence.

We have tried to summarize these additional elements of the *circuit of knowledge* in Figure 16.

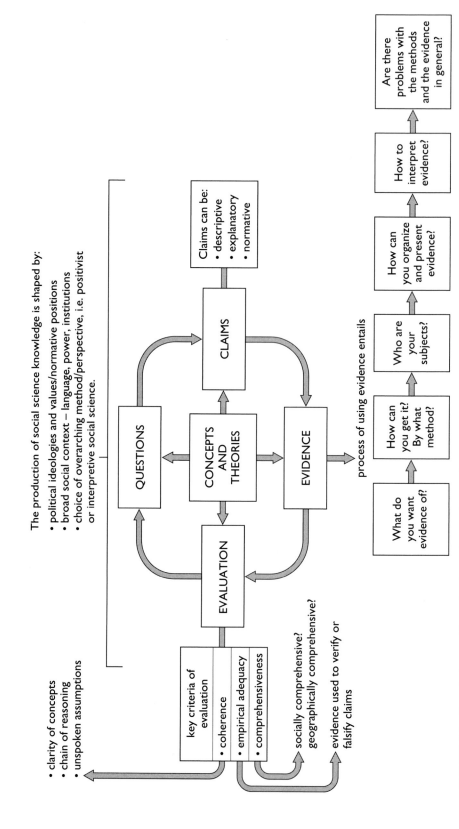

FIGURE 16 Knowledge and knowing: Introductory Block–Block 5 overview

Throughout DD100, we have argued that these kinds of issues and debates are best illuminated by using them, rather than considering them abstractly. So, in the rest of Section 5, we will be asking you to take these issues of *knowledge and knowing* and apply them first to the debates about the city and knowledge that you noted in Section 5.1, and then to some other materials from earlier in the course – which will provide you with a dry run for your work on TMA 06. This will also prepare you for much of your study on future social science courses, for many texts in the social sciences do not make their epistemological basis very clear – one has to dig it out from the text. Using the conceptual tools of *knowledge and knowing* in DD100 is a useful way of doing this.

There are many ways that you could approach this task and what is shown in Figure 17 is just one version for you to think about – though it will form the basis of your work in Section 5.3.

FIGURE 17   Extracting and evaluating the epistemological basis of social science arguments

(**1**)   What are the key questions being asked?

(**2**)   What are the key claims being made?

(**3**)   Is it possible to separate out descriptive, explanatory, and normative claims? Pause before moving on to evidence. Try and consider something of the social context of the argument and its theoretical origins.

(**4**)   Think carefully about the key concepts that the text appears to use. Do they cluster together? Do they appear to be implicitly or explicitly arranged in a theoretical framework? Ask yourself whether these concepts and theories have asked the most open set of questions. Have they also closed down options and created absences that should be investigated?

(**5**)   If it is not explicitly stated, can you work back from concepts, theory and the character of claims (especially any normative claims) to the wider social science context from which the arguments have sprung? Can you deduce the presence of any particular set of values, political ideologies, specific institutional origins, or overriding social science method/model: positivist or interpretive?

(**6**)   What evidence has been amassed to support and shape the argument? To which specific claims and questions does the evidence speak?

(**7**)   How was that evidence obtained, by whom, by what methods, and about what subject population?

(8) How has the evidence been presented, organized and interpreted? How have the initial concepts and theories shaped the selection and interpretation of evidence?

(9) Has the argument been evaluated? Has it been compared with any other arguments? What does the text itself claim?

(10) Can you apply the key tests of coherence, empirical adequacy, and comprehensiveness to the argument(s)?

(11) What new questions came out of the process of evaluation? How do the original claims fare, when examined?

(12) Overall, how has the broad social context and political values of the work shaped its internal detail?

5.3 Which way for cities?

ACTIVITY 24

Go back to your notes on Reading 11 (Cairncross) and Reading 12 (Reich) from Section 5.1 and the connections we made to other parts of the course.

Subject both the optimists and pessimists to the list of questions outlined above in Figure 17 and make new short notes.

Don't worry if not all the questions can be answered in great detail.

Then take a look at our notes below. But remember, applying the questions is the key to knowledge and knowing, so do have a go before you look at our version.

COMMENT

Our notes looked like this:

CAIRNCROSS – OPTIMISTS

1 Key questions

How will information technology/communications revolution (IT/CR) impact on cities?

NB. Question tends to frame whole issue in terms of technological change. What does this exclude?

2 and 3 Key claims: what types of claims?

(a) IT/CR → is in early stages, impact will increase

(b) IT → structured change in:

> home
> work
> travel patterns
> location decisions

(c) Combined together this will reinvent city centres

(d) On balance the impact will be positive, especially for young and well educated

Broadly (a) and (b) descriptive, (c) explanatory, (d) is normative.

4 Key concepts/theoretical frameworks

Key concepts

> IT/CR → Death of Distance
> irrelevance of space for social organization.

Theories

> post-industrialism – Bell
> theoretical knowledge
> knowledge economy/society – Leadbeater.

NB – Hall

> economies of scale
> agglomeration economics
> economies of inertia.

Theories

> Cairncross appears to be close to liberal models of the functioning and values of the flexible labour market (open to attack perhaps)

NB –

> see BK 5, Ch. 4, Sect. 5 on drawing out the theory.

5 Context/values/ideologies

Main context appears to be liberalism – assumptions about values of free market. Somewhat lack of concern about losers.

Very little mention of role of state in shaping these developments – focus on opportunities rather than constraints.

Does this lead Hall/Cairncross to ignore the kinds of evidence Reich et al. look at?

The central determining, law-like impact of IT/CR on social life – suggests a kind of positivism.

6-8 Evidence/methods/problems

As Cairncross projects into the future - evidence as yet awaits final judgement.

NOTE - much of the evidence on teleworking is drawn from research done by phone companies! Do they have an interest in producing research that favours teleworking?

Hall - focuses on successful cases (City of London/Silicon Valley) - but does this hide the cases of less successful cities?

9 and 10 Evaluation and criteria

See especially BK 5, Ch. 4, Sect. 5 on evaluation of post-industrialism/ knowledge economy arguments.

Coherence:	Some key concepts need unpacking especially determining link to concepts of power.
	Chain of reasoning runs into technological determinist problems. Limited role for agency, individual or collective.
	Unspoken assumptions. Liberalism especially unspoken but deeply enmeshed in construction of argument.
Empirical adequacy:	These readings too limited to provide significant verificationary evidence - though some evidence a bit questionable, strong on individual studies.
Comprehensiveness:	Very narrow range of cities considered, inadequate attention to role of politics and power.

11 and 12 New questions and context

Written at early stages of changes in communications technology, therefore a bit liable to hype, over dependence on technology arguments.

Implicit liberalism needs to be unpacked as it leads to over focus on purely economic dynamics/forces, lacks sense of power in economics.

New questions:

How do the structural powers of markets shape the introduction and deployment of new communication technologies?

How will this reshape cities geographically and socially?

REICH - PESSIMISTS

1 Key questions

Reich: Why do symbolic analysts/knowledge workers separate themselves from the rest of the public in US cities?

Sassen: What is the impact of the changing structure of the global economy on the economy and social structure of cities?

Worpole: Why has the quality of urban life, and the quality of public space on which it depends, been diminished in UK cities?

2 and 3 Key claims: what types of claims?

Reich: US cities are locked into vicious downward cycles of increasing fragmentation and inequality.

This is driven by inequalities in public and private provision and increasing inequalities in the labour market created by a knowledge economy.

Sassen: The globalization of economic activity has created the need for nodal centres of economic control - financial markets, banks, corporate HQs.

These concentrate in global cities, creating massive growth in high-income service sector jobs and low-income service provider jobs.

Worpole: Public space has been progressively degraded by car-dominated transport, the privatization of leisure facilities and out of town retailing. The worse it gets the more people withdraw, degrading it further.

4 Key concepts/theoretical frameworks

Reich's work draws on a kind of pessimistic globalist position (see BK 4, Ch. 1, Sect. 5) and a post-Fordist account of the labour market consequences of the new economy (BK 5, Ch. 4, Sect. 3.1).

Sassen's work is more closely connected to Marxism, evidenced in her use of key Marxist concepts (class, polarization, profit, value) and her emphasis on the dynamics of a competitive, profit-driven capitalist economy (BK 3, Ch. 3).

Worpole's work is harder to place as it is not concerned directly with either global forces or the knowledge economy, but see BK 2, Ch. 3 on transport, the market, and externalities and the social democratic critique of neo-classical models of the market.

5 Context/values/ideologies

Clear connections to ideological positions:

> Sassen elements of Marxism
>
> Reich social democratic
>
> Worpole social democratic – with a strong dose of environmentalism

Not surprising that there is more focus here on forms of inequality of wealth and power and less emphasis on pure technological determinism.

Does this approach lead writers to underestimate the virtues and successes of new cities/economies? Importance and value of individual choices despite social costs?

6-8 Evidence/methods/problems

A bit unfair to compare with optimists as readings do have greater range of evidence.

On their own terms, good mix of case studies, Reich stronger on quantitative data, Worpole too.

Sassen focused on just three cities and ones with very specific location in the global economy.

Reich's focus on US brings limits for our purposes, but the line of argument the evidence supports may be applicable to the UK in some cases.

9 and 10 Evaluation and criteria

Neo-Fordism and pessimistic globalizers evaluated in BK 5, Ch. 4, Sect. 5 and Workbook 5, Sect. 4, as well as Workbook 4, Sect. 5.

Coherence:	Who actually are the symbolic analysts? Are they really a separate class who act in unison? What unites them?
	Is there an over-reliance on the global and economic forces in exploring cities and changing character? What about politics/government? What about local differences and local resistance?
Empirical adequacy:	Clearly problems with US evidence for UK.
	Limits of global cities evidence.
	NB. Taylor's evidence – Manchester, Sheffield cases very useful balance.

11 and 12 New questions and context

Marxist/soc. dem./environmentalist theories and values clearly shape main lines of enquiry – leads to neglect of individual freedoms and experience, incline to pessimism.

New questions:

How could we replicate Reich's work for the UK?

How relevant are these arguments to smaller, newer UK cities?

How can we dig out and connect the vicious circle arguments embedded in Reich's and Worpole's work?

Working through course materials in this kind of way is precisely what we will be asking you to do in TMA 06 if you choose the option on *knowledge and knowing*.

We won't be doing any more analysis here, but we do want to alert you to some of the key debates and arguments in DD100 that would be most amenable to this kind of analysis. They are as follows.

Block 1	Accounting for changing economic identities – Chapter 3.
	Marx vs. Weber.
	Work vs. consumption identities.
	Social polarization and social exclusion.
	Contrasting models of nationalism – Chapter 4.
Block 2	Accounting for differences in human intelligence – Chapter 1.
	Neo-Darwinism US IQ testing vs. developmental psychology.
	Four models of health and illness – Chapter 2.
Block 3	Accounting for power – Weber vs. Foucault – the GM foods debate and teleworking.
	The impact of values and ideologies on social science arguments.
	Feminists and conservatives on the family – Chapter 2.
	Liberals, social democrats and Marxists on work – Chapter 3.
	All five ideologies on the welfare state – Chapter 4.
Block 4	Accounting for globalization. Globalists vs. traditionalists vs. transformationalists.
Block 5	Accounting for religion – Chapter 2.
	Positivists vs. interpretativists.
	Accounting for the knowledge society – Chapter 4.
	Post-industrialists vs. post-Fordists vs. risk society.

6 ASSESSING BLOCK 6

We've said enough. It's time to sign off and to wish you the best of luck with your final DD100 assessment.

 You should now turn to the *Assignments Booklet* for TMA 06.

C O M M E N T   O N   A C T I V I T Y   9 _____

Cities and globalization

	Sassen	Taylor
Global vs. local	Global more significant force than the local.	More weight given to local conditions and local peculiarities.
Models of globalization	Broadly globalist model with strong Marxist elements.	Transformationalist argument that emphasizes variability and newness.
Winners and losers	Global cities clearly winners over provincial cities, but massive inequalities within global cities.	Some cities win by reinvention, niche marketing (Manchester); others lose out (Sheffield).
Uncertainty and diversity		Old models of urban growth uncertain; diversity of urban responses to globalization created.
Structures	Global financial markets and flows. Multi-national corporations and networks of global production.	Importance of local cultural and infrastructural structures.
Agency	Limited role for agency outside of dominant economic actors.	Strong role for agency of local urban growth coalitions.

REFERENCES

Aitchison, J. and Carter, H. (2000) *Language, Economy and Society: The Changing Fortunes of the Welsh Language in the Twentieth Century*, Cardiff, University of Wales Press.

Cairncross, F. (1997) *The Death of Distance*, London, Orion.

Campbell, B. (1993) *Goliath: Britain's Dangerous Places*, London, Methuen.

Carter, H. (1995) *The Study of Urban Geography*, London, Arnold.

CBDC (1999) *Fact Sheet*, November, Cardiff Bay Development Corporation.

Champion, A.G. and Townsend, A.R. (1990) *Contemporary Britain: A Geographical Perspective*, London, Edward Arnold.

Cochrane, A. (1999) 'Administered cities' in Pile, S., Brook, C. and Mooney, G. (eds) *Unruly Cities?: Order/Disorder*, London, Routledge/The Open University.

Cox, A. (1984) *Adversary Politics and Land: The Conflict over Land and Property Policy in Post-War Britain*, Cambridge, Cambridge University Press.

Daunton, M.J. (1977) *Coal Metropolis, Cardiff, 1870–1914*, London, Leicester University Press.

Evans, C., Dodsworth, S. and Barnett, J. (1984) *Below the Bridge: A Photo-Historical Survey of Cardiff's Docklands to 1983*, Cardiff, Amgueddfa Genedlaethol Cymru.

Evans, N. (1985) 'The Welsh Victorian city: the middle class and civic and national consciousness in Cardiff, 1850–1914', *Welsh History Review*, vol.12, pp.350–87.

Fyfe, N. (1997) 'Crime' in Pacione, M. (ed.) *Britain's Cities: Geographies of Division in Urban Britain*, London, Routledge.

Gripaios, P., Gripaios, R. and Munday, M. (1997) 'The role of inward investment in urban economic development: the cases of Bristol, Cardiff and Plymouth', *Urban Studies*, vol.34, no.4, pp.579–603.

Hall, P. (1996) 'Cities of people and cities of bits' in Young, R. *et al.* (eds).

Hall, P., Thomas, R., Gracey, H. and Drewett, R. (1973) *The Containment of Urban England*, vol.2, London, George Allen and Unwin.

Hausner, V.A. (1987) *Urban Economic Change: Five City Studies*, Oxford, Clarendon Press.

Jordan, G. and Weedon, C. (1995) *Cultural Politics: Class, Gender, Race and the Postmodern World*, Oxford, Blackwell.

Lee, D. and Newby, H. (1983) *The Problem of Sociology*, London, Unwin Hyman.

McDowell, L. (1994) 'The transformation of cultural geography' in Gregory, D., Martin, R. and Smith, G. (eds) *Human Geography*, London, Macmillan.

Massey, D., Allen, J. and Pile, S. (eds) (1999) *City Worlds*, London, Routledge/The Open University.

Northedge, A. (1990) *The Good Study Guide*, Milton Keynes, The Open University.

O'Leary, P. (1998) 'Of devolution, maps and divided mentalities', *Planet*, no.127, pp.7–12.

Raban, J. (1974) *Soft City*, London, Hamish Hamilton.

Reich, R. (1991) *The Work of Nations: Preparing Ourselves for 21st-Century Capitalism*, London, Simon & Schuster.

Reith Report (1946) *New Towns Committee: Final Report*, Cmnd. 6876, London, HMSO.

Robson, B. (1988) *These Inner Cities*, Oxford, Clarendon Press.

Rogers, R. (1997) *Cities for a Small Planet*, London, Faber and Faber.

Sassen, S. (1991/1996) 'The global city' in Fainstein, S.S. and Campbell, S. (eds) *Readings in Urban Theory*, Oxford, Blackwell (first published as *The Global City*, Princeton, Princeton University Press).

Sherwood, M. (1991) 'Racism and resistance: Cardiff in the 1930s and 1940s', *Llafur*, vol.5, no.4, pp.51–70.

Taylor, I. (1996) 'Two tales of two cities' in Young, R. *et al.* (eds).

Thomas, H. (1992) 'Redevelopment in Cardiff Bay: state intervention and the securing of consent', *Contemporary Wales*, vol.5, pp.81–98.

Thomas, H. (1999) 'Spatial restructuring in the capital: struggles to shape Cardiff's built environment' in Fevre, R. and Thompson, A. (eds) *National Identity and Social Theory. Perspectives from Wales*, Cardiff, University of Wales Press.

Thomas, H. and Imrie, R. (1993) 'What's in a name?', *Planet*, no.10, pp.8–13.

Thomas, H., Stirling, T., Brownill, S. and Razzaque, K. (1996) 'Locality, urban governance and contested meanings of place', *Area*, vol.28, no.2, pp.186–98.

Trystan, D. (1997) 'Dosbarth, cymuned, cenedl … a threfn', *Barn*, no.147, pp.16–19.

Western Mail (1993) 'Capital aims for Europe top spot', 12 March, p.6.

Worpole, K. (1992) *Towns for People: Transforming Urban Life*, Buckingham, Open University Press.

Young, M. and Willmott, P. (1986) *Family and Kinship in East London*, Harmondsworth, Penguin.

Young, R. *et al.* (eds) (1996) *The Return of the Local*, Demos Quarterly, London, Demos.

ACKNOWLEDGEMENTS

Grateful acknowledgement is made to the following sources for permission to reproduce material in this review.

Text

Raban, J. (1974) *Soft City*, Hamish Hamilton. Copyright © Jonathan Raban, 1974; Rogers, R. (1997) *Cities for a Small Planet* (ed.) Gumuchdjian, P., Faber and Faber. Also by permission of Westview Press, Boulder, Colorado; Sassen, S. (1991) *The Global City*. Copyright © 1991 by Princeton University Press. Reprinted by permission of Princeton University Press; Taylor, I. (1996) 'Two tales of two cities', *Demos*, 9/1996; Hall, P. (1996) 'Cities of people and cities of bits', *Demos*, 9/1996; Young, M. and Willmott, P. (1986) *Family and Kinship in East London*, Routledge; Worpole, K. (1992) *Towns for People, Transforming Urban Life*, Open University Press; Fyfe, N. (1997) 'Crime', in Pacione, M. (ed.) *Britain's Cities, Geographies of Division in Urban Britain*, Routledge; Thomas, H., Stirling, T., Brownill, S. and Razzaque, K. (1996) 'Locality, urban governance and contested meanings of place', *Area*, vol.28, no.2, June 1996, pp.192–6, courtesy of the Royal Geographical Society; Cairncross, F. (1998) *The Death of Distance: How the Communications Revolution Will Change Our Lives*, Texere Publishing Ltd; Reich, R. (1991) *The Work of Nations: Preparing Ourselves for 21st-Century Capitalism*. Copyright © Robert R. Reich, 1991. Reprinted by permission of Simon and Schuster Ltd and the Sagalyn Literary Agency, Bethesda, MD.

Figures

Figure 4: Hall, P. (1992) *Urban and Regional Planning*, Routledge; Figure 10.2: Anderson, S., Smith, C.G., Kinsey, R. and Wood, J. (1990) *The Edinburgh Crime Survey: First Report*, Scottish Office Central Research Unit; Figures 7, 12 and 13: By permission of Cardiff Bay Development Corporation; Figure 8: Aitchison, J. and Carter, H. (2000) *Language, Economy and Society: The Changing Fortunes of the Welsh Language in the Twentieth Century*, University of Wales Press; Figure 9: O'Leary, P. (1998) 'Of devolution, maps and divided mentalities, deconstructing a new national icon', *Planet*, no.127, Berw Cyf, © Paul O'Leary 1998; Figure 10: Adapted from Thomas, H. (1992) 'Redevelopment in Cardiff Bay: state intervention and the securing of consent', *Contemporary Wales*, vol.5, University of Wales Press; Figure 11: © National Museums and Galleries of Wales; Figure 14: Front cover of residents' newspaper *Making Waves*, January 2000, issue no.112, by permission of NewEmploy Wales Ltd. Photo: John Sinclair.

Tables

Table 3: Carter, H. (1995) *The Study of Urban Geography*, Edward Arnold; Table 4: Champion, A.G. and Townsend, A.R. (1990) *Contemporary Britain, A Geographical Perspective*, Edward Arnold; Table 5: Begg, I. and Eversley, D. (1986) 'Deprivation in the inner city: social indicators from the 1981 census', *Critical Issues in Urban Economic Development*, vol.1, Clarendon Press. By permission of Oxford University Press; Table 7: Office for National Statistics (2000), © Crown Copyright is reproduced with the permission of the Controller of Her Majesty's Stationery Office; Tables 8, 9 and 10: Office for National Statistics (1991) *Census 1991*. © Crown Copyright is reproduced with the permission of the Controller of Her Majesty's Stationery Office; Table 10.5: Mirrlees-Black, C. and Aye Maung, N. (1994) *Fear of Crime: Findings From the 1992 British Crime Survey*, Home Office Research and Statistics Department, Research Findings No.9; Table 10.6: Kinsey, R. and Anderson, A. (1992) *Crime and the Quality of Life: Public Perceptions and Experiences of Crime in Scotland – Findings from the 1988 British Crime Survey*, Scottish Office Central Research Unit.

Illustration

p.31: Le Corbusier (1987) *The City of Tomorrow*, Butterworth-Heinemann Ltd, © FLC/ADAGP, Paris and DACS, London 2000.

Cover

STUDY SKILLS INDEX